Delicious Words

As societies across the globe are becoming increasingly interwoven at an unprecedented speed and across an impressive scope, so too is the world of food, allowing the English language to develop an ever-widening culinary vocabulary. This book examines the lives of such words in today's discourse on eating and drinking, focusing on foreign – particularly East Asian – influences on culinary terms in English, and how words are born and evolve in a modern transcultural environment. Through the lens of culinary words, this book demonstrates that foreign-origin and hybrid words, previously considered marginal, have become a main source of new imports into our daily lexicon.

With case studies from Japan to Mongolia, Hong Kong to Korea, China to Vietnam, and beyond, this book examines how more and more words are becoming borderless and forming their own new global identities. By showcasing some lesser-known regional cuisines, alongside staple dishes that many of us already know and love, this book offers a wide range of examples in order to illustrate the metamorphosis of the manner in which we engage with food words.

This book will be of interest to general readers, as well as those who are engaged in East Asian studies, English linguistics, intercultural communication studies, translation studies, and lexicography.

Jieun Kiaer is an Associate Professor of Korean Language and Linguistics at the University of Oxford. Her research interests include the formation of translingual/transcultural words and dynamic lexicons. She is particularly interested in the role of social media in the global lexicon. Kiaer is the series editor for Routledge Studies in East Asian Translation and has most recently published *Translingual Words* (Routledge, 2019).

Routledge Studies in East Asian Translation
Series Editors: Jieun Kiaer, University of Oxford, UK
Amy Xiaofan Li, University College London, UK

Routledge Studies in East Asian Translation aims to discuss issues and challenges involved in translation between Chinese, Japanese and Korean as well as from these languages into European languages with an eye to comparing the cultures of translation within East Asia and tracking some of their complex interrelationships.

Most translation theories are built on translation between European languages, with only few exceptions. However, this Eurocentric view on language and translation can be seriously limited in explaining the translation of non-European literature and scholarship, especially when it comes to translating languages outside the Indo-European family that have radically different script forms and grammatical categories, and may also be embedded in very different writing traditions and cultures. This series considers possible paradigm shifts in translation theory, arguing that translation theory and practice need to go beyond European languages and encompass a wider range of literature and scholarship.

Translation and Literature in East Asia
Between Visibility and Invisibility
Jieun Kiaer, Jennifer Guest, and Xiaofan Amy Li

Korean Literature Through the Korean Wave
Jieun Kiaer and Anna Yates-Lu

Delicious Words
East Asian Food Words in English
Jieun Kiaer

For more information about this series, please visit: www.routledge.com/languages/series/RSEAT

Delicious Words
East Asian Food Words in English

Jieun Kiaer

LONDON AND NEW YORK

First published 2021
by Routledge
2 Park Square, Milton Park, Abingdon, Oxon OX14 4RN

and by Routledge
52 Vanderbilt Avenue, New York, NY 10017

Routledge is an imprint of the Taylor & Francis Group, an informa business

© 2021 Jieun Kiaer

The right of Jieun Kiaer to be identified as author of this work has been asserted by her in accordance with sections 77 and 78 of the Copyright, Designs and Patents Act 1988.

All rights reserved. No part of this book may be reprinted or reproduced or utilised in any form or by any electronic, mechanical, or other means, now known or hereafter invented, including photocopying and recording, or in any information storage or retrieval system, without permission in writing from the publishers.

Trademark notice: Product or corporate names may be trademarks or registered trademarks, and are used only for identification and explanation without intent to infringe.

British Library Cataloguing-in-Publication Data
A catalogue record for this book is available from the British Library

Library of Congress Cataloging-in-Publication Data
Names: Kiaer, Jieun, author.
Title: Delicious words: East Asian food words in English / Jieun Kiaer.
Description: New York: Routledge, 2020. |
Series: Routledge studies in East Asian translation |
Includes bibliographical references and index.
Identifiers: LCCN 2020006865 (print) | LCCN 2020006866 (ebook) |
ISBN 9780367337704 (hardback) | ISBN 9780429321801 (ebook)
Subjects: LCSH: English language—Foreign words and phrases. |
Cooking—East Asia—Terminology. |
Ethnic food—East Asia—Terminology.
Classification: LCC PE1582.A3 K53 2020 (print) |
LCC PE1582.A3 (ebook) | DDC 428.1—dc23
LC record available at https://lccn.loc.gov/2020006865
LC ebook record available at https://lccn.loc.gov/2020006866

ISBN: 978-0-367-33770-4 (hbk)
ISBN: 978-0-367-50591-2 (pbk)
ISBN: 978-0-429-32180-1 (ebk)

Typeset in Times New Roman
by codeMantra

Contents

List of figures	vi
List of tables	viii
Preface	ix
Acknowledgements	xi
Introduction	1
1 Food words as translingual words	12
2 Early encounters: first-generation food words	26
3 Fusion, localisation, and hybridity: second-generation food words	54
4 Globalisation and social media: the global food words	71
5 New words as cultural capital	104
Bibliography	129
Index	133

Figures

I.1	Three Es model	7
1.1	Examples of 'sweet and sour' being used in different languages on Twitter	17
1.2	Example of *vegan bulgogi* on Twitter	18
1.3	A bowl of 親子丼 (oyakodon, 'parent-and-child rice bowl')	23
2.1	Graph showing transition from use of Peking to Beijing, 1800–2000	37
2.2	Boomerang word *beeru* on Twitter	39
2.3	Boomerang word *katsu* on Twitter	40
2.4	*Tsamba* on Twitter	45
2.5	*Matcha* on Twitter	47
2.6	*Pho* in different languages on Twitter	52
3.1	*Somaek* on Twitter	59
3.2	*Phojito* on Twitter	60
3.3	'QQ' on Twitter	64
3.4	'Milk tea' in Global Web-Based English (GloWbE)	66
3.5	*Bibimbap* salad on Twitter	67
3.6	'Chinese Tapas' on Twitter	68
3.7	Shrimp *Twigim* on Twitter	69
3.8	'Sushi burrito' on Twitter	69
4.1	'Peking duck' in Turkish- and Russian-language tweets	79
4.2	Food-related emojis on iPhone	80
4.3	Food-related emojis on Samsung Galaxy	81
4.4	Emoji substituting for words	81
4.5	Food image sharing on Twitter	82
4.6	Ainu cuisine on Twitter	84
4.7	Minority cuisines of China on Twitter	85
4.8	Uighur cuisine on Twitter	85
4.9	Variant spelling of *bibimbap* on Twitter	86

List of figures   vii

4.10 The finely grained distinction between *ramyen*
       and *ramen* on Twitter   87
4.11 *Katsu* in international culinary contexts   88
4.12 Korean *donkasu* on social media   89
4.13 *Bokkeum* on Twitter   90
4.14 Calqued term 'knife cut noodles' on Twitter   91
4.15 Google N-gram results for 'dumpling', 'gyoza',
       'jiaozi', and 'mandu', English Corpus, 1800–2000   92
4.16 #*guotie* on Twitter   93
4.17 #*jiaozi* on Twitter   93
4.18 Instagram results for Jamaican #dumplings   94
4.19 Google N-gram results for 'dumpling', English
       corpus, 1500–2008   96
4.20 Post from the Facebook group Subtle Asian
       Traits debating terms for 'bubble tea'   97
4.21 Post from the Facebook group Subtle Asian
       Traits debating terms for 'bubble tea'   98
5.1   Coca-Cola can in Kobe, Japan   107
5.2   McDonald's (マクドナルドハンバーガー,
       makudonarudo hanbāgā) restaurant in Tokyo, Japan   108
5.3   Spam (스팸, *Seupaem*) gift set on sale in Busan,
       South Korea   109
5.4   Pizza Hut (ピザハット, *pizahatto*) delivery moped
       in Kobe, Japan   109
5.5   Drinks menu featuring Red Bull (红牛, *hóngniú*)
       in Shanghai, China   111
5.6   Starbucks Coffee (星巴克咖啡 *xīng bākè kāfēi*)
       shop in Shanghai, China   112
5.7   Burger King (漢堡王, *hànbǎo wáng*) shop in
       Hsinchu, Taiwan   113
5.8   Imported Chinese tea in Leiden, the Netherlands   115
5.9   *BASICHOUSE MAN* – English-language
       branding of a South Korean company at a mall
       in Chengdu, China   118
5.10 *Bobocorn* – popcorn in Chengdu, China   120
5.11 Bread with English, Chinese, and Japanese
       branding in Shanghai, China   121
5.12 Poster at a fast food stand in Shanghai, China   122
5.13 Trilingual signage in English, Korean, and Chinese   122
5.14 Instant coffee packet in Shanghai, China   123
5.15 Drink packaging with multiple languages in
       Shanghai, China   124
5.16 French-influenced bottled water in Shanghai, China   125

Tables

I.1 Common English food words of foreign origin (OED)   2
2.1 East Asian-origin words in the Duden   41

Preface

Have you ever heard of a *sushi burrito*? Is it possible to have *boba* without *boba*? Do you consider *dumpling* to be a Chinese word, English word, or something else? What is the meaning of the word *vaganuary*? Is it a word or not? This book delves deep into the interactions and evolution of food words – a transnational, transcultural, and translingual phenomenon. I aim to describe how the forms, meanings, and identities of food words with East Asian roots are constantly in flux in our ever-diversified world, which is also mediated via global languages like English. Words receive new meanings, new forms, and new identities from their worldwide users. This process is sped up by the use of social media and the growth in the popularity of the English language worldwide. It is noticeable that the meanings, forms, and identities of these words are not determined by some kind of linguistic authorities, but rather constantly negotiated by common people. This book adopts the notion of *translanguaging* (García and Wei, 2014) as a conceptual foundation with which to explain the dynamic, borderless, creative, and transformative processes of meaning-making in the food word lexicon. This observation, however, can be stretched beyond food words.

With case studies from Japan to Mongolia, Hong Kong to Korea, China to Vietnam, and beyond, this book examines how more and more words are becoming borderless and forming their own new global identities. By showcasing some lesser-known regional cuisines, alongside staple dishes that many of us already know and love, this book offers a wide range of examples in order to illustrate the metamorphosis of the manner in which we engage with food words. The role of social media is now at the forefront of this change, where everyday online users can be considered participants and even pioneers in shaping the culinary lexicon. In an increasingly interconnected society, the ways in which we understand and use food words are rapidly transforming. Linguistic freedom and creativity are allowed – even encouraged to

x *Preface*

an extent. The exciting realms of East Asian food and language are brought into dialogue through this book. With this book I hope to provide an accessible and mouth-watering read that will whet your linguistic appetite and leave you hungry for more.

Acknowledgements

I am very grateful to Niamh Calway, Alexandra Kimmons, Toby Bladen, Amena Nebres, and Eleanor Wyllie for the invaluable help they have provided at the every stage of this project. I would also like to thank Young Bin Min Trust Fund and John Fell Fund for the support in completing the book.

Introduction

Culinary words of foreign origin are increasing and thriving in the English language, and the forms and meanings of these words reflect the transcultural nature of terms relating to food. This book explores the diversity of the forms (types of romanisation, transliteration, translation, and so on), identities, and meanings of these terms in World English(es). The influence of social media has made this process much more complex and diverse. This observation is in line with Eckert's (2012) discussion of the 'third wave' of sociolinguistic theory, in which speakers use various styles, including word choice, to situate themselves in the social landscape. In addition, I argue that the availability of multiple words in the English language to express the same concept allows speakers a greater expressive range that serves to enhance lexical power and becomes a form of cultural capital (Hills, 2002). In the following chapters, I shall present case studies on how English is being reshaped, rejuvenated, and made more 'delicious' by other languages and cultures. This introduction outlines some of the necessary conceptual foundations for this discussion.

I.1 Foreign food words in English

The English language contains food and drink terms from diverse sources. Foreign food terms are born through cultural interaction and are used not only by specialists but also among the general public. Foreign food words settle into English relatively quickly, often without retaining any trace of foreignness. For instance, *tea* is often associated with British culture, but the term itself originated in China. In the same way, *marmalade*, a popular fruit preserve in the UK and the favourite food of the iconic children's literature character *Paddington Bear,* is commonly associated with Britishness. However, the term *marmalade* has a foreign origin; while the titular character in the *Paddington Bear*

2 Introduction

Table I.1 Common English food words of foreign origin (OED)

Item	Etymology
Bacon	Germanic; entered English via Old French
Broccoli	Italian
Carrot	Greek; entered Latin and passed to French, then entered English
Celery	Greek; passed through a dialect of Italian to French and finally into English
Chocolate	Nahuatl; entered English via Spanish
Chutney	Hindi
Coffee	Arabic; entered English via Turkish
Ketchup	Perhaps Malay; borrowed into English from Hokkien Chinese
Marmalade	Greek; entered Latin and passed to descendant, Portuguese, then entered English
Noodle	German
Potato	A Central American Indian language; entered English via Spanish
Tomato	Nahuatl; entered English via Spanish
Yoghurt	Ottoman Turkish

stories came to the UK from Peru, the word *marmalade* actually entered English through the Portuguese language, attested by its entry into the Oxford English Dictionary (OED) as *marmelada* in 1521.[1] Similarly, the *potato*, a staple in traditional British cooking, originally came from the Americas. The OED states that the earliest form of the word – *batata* – comes from a Central American Indian language. The term was borrowed by Spanish colonists in 1526 as *patata*, before finally making its way into the English language as *potato*. In addition to the *potato*, *carrot* and *broccoli* are in fact also foreign-origin words; *carrot* entered English via French, and *broccoli* via Italian. These examples, just a small selection of a vast number of words, illustrate how terms from other languages have been fully absorbed into British language and culture. Table I.1 shows some of the British staple food names which are of foreign origin.

I.2 Growth of East Asian food words in English

For a long time, many scholars were sceptical about the impact of East Asian words on the English lexicon. However, as I shall discuss throughout the book, the situation is changing. East Asian food terms are rapidly increasing in the English language, and reshaping the English lexicon. As well as growing in sheer number, they sometimes challenge the meanings and forms of existing words, and create new linguistic currency. For instance, as we shall see in Chapter 2, words such as *dumpling* or *noodle* are now predominantly used within the context of Asian, rather than Western, cuisine. This process of word-making and sharing is becoming more dynamic and lively due to the growth of worldwide social media (Chapter 4). Internationalisation of the English language has also diversified the routes through which East Asian words enter English. For instance, many K-pop or J-pop related words enter the English language not through its US and UK varieties, but through Southeast Asian varieties of the language (Kiaer, 2019).

I.3 Internationalisation of the English language: English in East Asia

Kachru (1985) famously summarised the situation of English in different regions of the world in his World Englishes model, dividing them into the 'Inner Circle', spoken in places where English is a native language (such as the UK, the USA, Australia, Canada, and New Zealand); 'Outer Circle', where English is a second language (such as India, Singapore, and Ghana); and 'Expanding Circle', where English is a foreign language (such as Korea, Japan, China, Israel, and Indonesia). For Kachru, countries in the Inner Circle represented the canonically privileged users, who comprised the traditional cultural and linguistic bases of English; and countries in the Outer Circle represented institutionalised non-native varieties of English, having passed through extended periods of colonisation. Countries in the Expanding Circle represented regions where the language is performed in English as a Foreign Language (EFL) contexts. However, as English becomes a global lingua franca and the number of speakers is constantly increasing, this hierarchical and prejudiced view of English must be challenged. We should also note the growing complexity and diversity of Inner Circle Englishes, as much of the population in these regions is rapidly becoming multilingual. The Asian influence in particular is growing. In the UK 2011 Census, the Asian or Asian British ethnic group category showed one of the largest increases since 2001, with a third of the foreign-born population of the UK (2.4 million) now identifying as Asian British (Office for National Statistics, 2013). Meanwhile, the number of people who learn English as a second language is growing more quickly than ever in East Asia. Unless otherwise stated, this book uses the term 'English' to refer to international varieties of English (Crystal, 2000) or World Englishes, instead of exclusively referring to Inner Circle varieties of English such as UK or US Englishes.

I.4 Defining East Asia

Before we discuss the nature of the East Asian-origin culinary words entering English, we need to define East Asia. East Asia refers to a region in the eastern part of the Eurasian continent. It has been defined either solely based on geographical features, or through the identification of a group of nation-states that have a strong degree of cultural overlap. The United Nations Statistical Division has provided an influential definition of *Eastern Asia* on a geographical and political basis, holding that the category includes: The People's Republic of China (PRC), alongside its Special Administrative Regions of Hong Kong and Macao; the Democratic People's Republic of Korea (North Korea); Japan; Mongolia; and the Republic of Korea (South Korea).[2] The Republic of China (ROC) is not recognised by the UN. The areas currently administered by the ROC government, such as the island of Taiwan, are considered to be located in Eastern Asia, but as a sub-region of the PRC. The ROC's precise status in international organisations like the UN is a sensitive and often emotive topic in East Asian politics.

East Asia has also been defined based on shared culture and history, with a reduced emphasis on geographical factors. Specifically, scholars refer to an 'East Asian Cultural Sphere' or 'Sinosphere' of cultures that were profoundly influenced by Han Chinese culture and Chinese character-writing. There is a clear consensus that this sphere contains not only China but also Japan and Korea. Additionally, definitions on the basis of shared culture often include Vietnam, considered part of South-Eastern Asia by the UN's more geographical definition, because of its long history of writing Chinese characters, which are known as Chữ Hán in Vietnamese. Cultural definitions of East Asia may or may not exclude the state of Mongolia. Mongolia is perhaps a borderline case in that there was extensive historical contact between the Mongolian and Han Chinese cultures, but Chinese character-writing was never fully adopted. Instead, the Mongolian language was historically written in its own traditional script, although the Cyrillic alphabet is now predominantly used in the modern state of Mongolia. The definition of East Asia on the basis of shared Sinitic culture is further complicated by the fact that countries with sizeable populations of overseas Chinese, such as Singapore or Malaysia, are universally excluded. If the definition of East Asia was based solely on the presence of Chinese cultural influences, we might expect these states to be included as well.

For the purposes of this book on food words, I did not feel it necessary to take an exclusive position on whether East Asia should be defined geographically or culturally. Instead, I adopted an inclusive view of East Asia that incorporates all regions from both the conventional geographical and cultural definitions. I will discuss the cuisine of Mongolia but also that of Vietnam, in addition to mainland China, Hong Kong, Macau, Taiwan, Japan, and the Korean peninsula.

I.5 Defining East Asian cuisine: diversity and commonality

The East Asian region is geographically large, densely populated, and culturally diverse. Accordingly, the region offers a broad range of different methods for preparing food. The term 'East Asian cuisine' is thus an umbrella term that covers the many cooking styles that are popular in modern East Asian countries. In this book, I adopt a territory-by-territory approach, treating the cuisine of mainland China as separate from that of Hong Kong, and both of these as separate from Japanese cooking. I believe this to be an effective way of making sure the diversity of the region is explored in suitable depth. Nevertheless, there are some limitations to this approach. First, these territories may contain indigenous minorities or sub-regions with their own food cultures that could equally be treated separately. Examples include the distinctive food cultures of the Ainu people of Japan, or the Sichuan region of mainland China. In order to account for this limitation, I will intentionally make explicit the internal diversity within each territory during my discussion. Equally, there are similarities across numerous cultures of East Asia when it comes to food preparation that extend beyond territorial lines. For example, many East Asian cuisines feature rice as a staple. This indicates that there are elements of East Asian cuisine which could potentially be generalised, without needing to divide discussion into different territories. As a result of this limitation, I will adopt a comparative approach in this book, identifying both the similarities and differences between different East Asian cuisines when appropriate. In this way, I seek to strike a balance in placing each cuisine in its appropriate internal and external context.

I.6 Methodologies

This book presents textual and multimodal examples from diverse offline and online sources, incorporating evidence gathered through online databases such as ProQuest, Nexis, JSTOR, Google Books,

6 *Introduction*

and GloWbE. ProQuest, JSTOR, and Google Books hold a massive collection of journals and ebooks, while Nexis holds a similar database of (digital) newspapers from all over the world that can be cross-referenced when searching for keywords. GloWbE is a corpus of Global Web-Based English that tracks online lexicon in various geographical locations. Filtering through these online databases for keywords has a twofold objective – not only does this method seek out evidence of widespread use of individual words in their English forms, and provide dates for the first recorded instance that words were used in print, but it also attempts to recognise *how* words are being used, determining where they fit in the different parts of speech used in English, such as determining whether they are used as a noun, adjective, conjunction, interjection, and so on.

Evidence from social media also plays an important role in this book. This study uses social media to trace the online lives of target words. My method for working with social media uses content analysis of comments featuring selected words on popular social media platforms, with an emphasis on Twitter. Twitter is open to the general public for academic purposes, and no identifiable information has been included in Tweets featured in this study. As Twitter allows users to search by hashtag and features accurate time stamping for each Tweet, I was able to track any potential linguistic developments over the past ten years. Since less social media data is available pre-2008, I use data from 2008 to the present. I also use Google Trends and Google N-gram in order to trace the lives of food words in many varieties of English, not only Inner Circle varieties. Google N-gram is used to track the frequency of individual words, and Google Trends analyses their use in recent years, and compares pairs of words. As we shall explore, many subcultural food words born in East Asia have entered World English through Southeast Asian varieties of English. Making use of Google Trends and Google N-gram can help assess these usages in varieties of English found in the Outer or Expanding Circles of English speakers as they become increasingly important in the diversification of the English lexicon. In addition to the OED for British English, I will look at evidence from the Macquarie dictionary for Australian English, and the Merriam-Webster dictionary for US English.

I.7 First-, second-, and global generation words

Kiaer and Bordilovskaya (2017) have proposed a classification of Korean-English words into three groups: first-generation words,

Introduction 7

second-generation words, and global words. The terms and classifications used for words reflect how members of the diaspora settle in a new homeland. This book adopts the same classification to describe and explain diverse East Asian words in the English language. First-generation words can simply be understood as East Asian-born words that entered English. Most East Asian-origin words that entered the English language before the twentieth century belong to this category (Chapter 2). Second-generation words are those which, like second-generation immigrants, are born locally and contain at least some English elements. These are hybrid words with both English and Asian elements. Although they are often received negatively by linguistic authorities, they are considered valuable assets by local users (Chapter 3). Finally, as the Asian diaspora and their cultural influence continue to grow rapidly in tandem with global trade between East Asia and the English-speaking world, many locally made East Asian words have started to be used in a global English context. The second-generation words which surpass exclusive use in their local context are known as global words (Chapters 4 and 5).

I.8 Motivations in communication choices: efficiency, expressivity, and empathy

The making and sharing of words represents people's diverse communication needs and motivations. Kiaer and Han (2019) propose the three Es model shown in Figure I.1 to explain that there are three motivations and intrinsic desires in human communication: (i) efficiency, (ii) expressivity, and (iii) empathy. These motives guide word users to find the appropriate word and its form in each situation. Word users will consider all three when choosing and using words. I adopt this

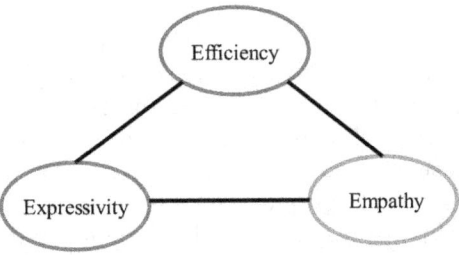

Figure I.1 Three Es model.

view in explaining the lexical decisions individuals make when adapting and using foreign-origin food words.

(i) Efficiency: Words are chosen to increase communicative efficiency.
(ii) Expressivity: Words are chosen for expressive power – to capture the nuanced nature of meaning(s) appropriate to the given context.
(iii) Empathy: Words are chosen to convey empathy and build solidarity between the word users and their audience.

i. Efficiency

Efficiency matters in communication. It is important to choose and use words that can be efficiently communicated to the audience. Based on Ziphian law, Kiaer (2014b) argues that efficient forms of human communication aim to maximise output, with minimised linguistic input. If a short, simple word can make the communication successful, then very little needs to be said. The efficiency motivation is in line with the Gricean maxim and cooperative principles in pragmatics (Grice, 1975). To take an example, two people who have lived in Vietnam and know Vietnamese cuisine well can use Vietnamese terms without translation while speaking in English. This is an efficient choice. However, if one of them does not know anything about the Vietnamese cuisine or language, then it is better to use English translations for communicative efficiency.

ii. Expressivity

People also consider their expressive desires when choosing the right word. Kiaer (2019a) showed that for South Koreans, choosing local Korean words evokes feelings of innocence and novelty, whereas the choice of Sino-origin words brings a sense of seriousness and sincerity. In recent years, Korean words for both dish names and ingredient names have been increasing in the English language. For instance, in Korean *ojingeo* (오징어) is used to refer to squid and *haemul* (해물) is used to refer to seafood. These ingredient words already exist in English languages, and there are no noticeable semantic differences. However, people use these local terms to express their desire to taste and experience different cuisines and cultures. For example, in a Korean restaurant someone may order a seafood pancake using the transliterated form *haemul pajeon,* even if the English translation is also on the menu. Sometimes, by using the original transliterated form, one can perceive an added value of authenticity. Such added meanings are often subjective and context-based.

Of course, the decision to use local terms that are particularly unfamiliar to the general public can make communication difficult to understand. In addition to word choices, the pronunciation or spelling of those words can also be influenced by multiple factors. You, Kiaer, and Ahn (2019) report that some British University students have negative attitudes towards using the original pronunciation of East Asian origin words: the students mentioned that it was confusing, unnecessary, and pretentious to pronounce them authentically, and was more natural to pronounce the words using English pronunciation norms. However, some students believed the words should be pronounced according to their language of origin because "it's more respectful to pronounce words according to their original pronunciation, if you can" and "nativized pronunciation is confusing". They also said they tried not to pronounce words with a strong English accent "as this might be offensive".

iii. Empathy

This motivation echoes a well-known quote from Mandela: "If you talk to a man in a language he understands, that goes to his head. If you talk to him in his language, that goes to his heart". Empathy and solidarity building is another important factor behind choosing the right form of a word. This is important particularly for a diaspora community or linguistic minority. Sharing culinary words and culture is like sharing experiences, life paths, and identities. For example, someone may call family members with whom they otherwise speak English by foreign-origin terms referring to specific familial relations, such as 'Eomma' (엄마 *eomma*, 'mum') or 'Shushu' (叔叔 *shūshu,* 'uncle'). This reinforces the feeling of shared heritage. This can also apply to food terms, as food is closely tied to family and memory. People may refer to dishes which have established English translations by their original name because that was the term used by their mother or grandmother; calling it by the same name may remind them of their family and bring them comfort. This can be especially true for diaspora members who may feel otherwise disconnected from heritage cultures and languages.

I.9 Core themes

In this book, I present the case studies of Japan, Korea, mainland China, Hong Kong, Macau, Vietnam, and Mongolia. For many of these countries, the meaningful encounters with the West began in the late nineteenth century, during a period of widespread colonisation by European powers, and this colonial history is reflected in the birth of transcultural, translingual culinary terms. For example, in Macau there is a Portuguese influence on food terms, and a French influence can be seen in Vietnamese culinary words. I aim to show how the complex and diverse history of each region gave rise to the various ways in which food words are introduced, made, and shared in a dynamic manner both locally and globally, particularly by ordinary people rather than linguistic authorities.

Additionally, I will discuss how factors like degree of exposure to Western culture, and usage of social media affect the transmission of culinary terms into English. This can go some way towards explaining, for example, why there are no words from Mongolian cuisine in the OED, as this area has historically had less contact with English-speaking cultures. In the nineteenth and twentieth centuries, when the general public's contact with the English-speaking world was more limited, the transmission of words to and from East Asia was relatively slow. This is no longer the case. In today's world, lexical interaction is extremely active on account of the speed of globalisation, and food words are no exception to this rule. Now, lexical interactions are dynamic and interactive, with hybrid terms becoming more common among culinary terms. The ways in which words are born have become truly diversified; it is by no means the case that all terms are simply transliterated or translated. The usage of food terms depends on the target audience, with nuance mattering a great deal, as observed in social media (Chapter 4) and in matters of global branding (Chapter 5).

Another important theme I address is romanisation. As there are numerous native writing systems in use in East Asia, it can be difficult to express the phonetic values of these languages using only the Roman alphabet. Even in the case of Vietnamese, which uses a form of the Roman alphabet due to influence from the former French colonial presence, the alphabet has been adapted with diacritics to reflect the tones present in the language. When these Vietnamese culinary terms are borrowed into English, the tone markers are sometimes stripped away in the process of Anglicisation. For example, the Vietnamese noodle soup dish *phở* is often presented without diacritics as simply *pho* in the UK. In the past, each country in East Asia had a strict policy of adherence to a specific method of romanisation. However, in the current social media era where anyone and everyone can be a publisher, there is no realistic way to control how language users romanise their words. I will show that style and context matter when opting for a specific romanised form. New words can be used as cultural assets (Bourdieu, 1985) and culinary fans often freely pick and choose different ways to represent their words of choice (see Chapters 4 and 5).

This book will explain how the journey of culinary words is often complex, meaning that words cannot always be explained with single or even dual linguistic origins. Instead, I argue that such words are better understood as *translingual words*, representing transcultural, global cuisine (Chapter 1). Kiaer (2019a) introduces the term *translingual words* to describe travelling words with a complex origin whose forms, meanings, and identities are established beyond nation-state language boundaries. This book discusses the birth and growth of food words that are increasingly becoming translingual. I also unmask the different layers of lexical interaction, and the ways in which food words are born and evolve in different linguistic environments. Even if the cultural origin of a food is from one country, its native language cannot decide how it is represented in new target languages.

Notes

1 In this book, I use the term OED to refer to the Oxford English Dictionary Third Edition.
2 https://unstats.un.org/unsd/methodology/m49/.

1 Food words as translingual words

This chapter explains the processes through which food words with East Asian heritage gain new status as English words and become *translingual words*. Most of these words are the nouns and names referring to a dish or sauce, but some are verbs or adjectives that show ways of cooking or manners of eating or drinking. These words reveal a complex and diverse history of language contact in each region, particularly with local languages and English.

In this text I look at East Asian culinary terms, the relationship between East Asia and the English-speaking world, and what this relationship has produced within the formation of the English lexicon. As mentioned in the Introduction, I will adopt an inclusive view of East Asia, focusing on the cuisine of Japan, Korea, mainland China, Hong Kong, Macau, Vietnam, and Mongolia.

International trade and, most dramatically, nineteenth- and twentieth-century imperialism and colonialism have played crucial roles in lexical exchange. Colonialism forcefully imposed language usage on people but, in most cases, they continued to speak their original language in the home and other settings. This created an environment ideally suited for lexical interaction and vocabulary sharing. After the end of the colonial period, the vocabularies in local languages remained irreversibly intertwined (Schneider, 2007). Nowadays, the process of word exchange has become extremely fast and complex, often involving multiple parties around the globe. This reflects our demographic reality: every corner of this world is now connected through the web, and the number of global travellers and migrants has increased dramatically.

It is difficult to find any formal theory or model to explain the diverse patterns of growth experienced by the East Asian-origin words discussed in this book. For example, Schneider's (2007) dynamic model is clearly and exclusively geared towards what he calls Postcolonial

Englishes (PCEs), namely, the Englishes that arose as the products of colonisation. While this theory is suited to territories such as Hong Kong, it struggles to offer an explanation for words from many other parts of East Asia.

This chapter therefore challenges, and demonstrates the limits of, the traditional terms such as *loan* or *borrowing* in lexicography and adopts the new term *translingual words* suggested by Kiaer (2019a). The words I focus on reveal that the motives for using foreign-origin words are much more diverse than ever before. Following Eckert's (2012) discussion of the 'third wave' of sociolinguistic theory, I propose that our choice of words and how we use them depend on individuals' styles and preferences rather than their birth languages.[1] I argue that in our globalised, multilingual era, one's semiotic repertoire for the choice and uses of words cannot be defined within the tenet of 'birth language', since the words in our lexicon easily reveal *translanguaging* behaviours that go beyond and between languages (García and Wei, 2014). In this chapter, I will explore the concept of *translingual words*, how they are made, and their forms, meanings, and identities.

1.1 Beyond borrowing: birth of translingual words

Lexical migration and interaction are increasing. There are two kinds of lexical borrowing: cultural borrowing and core borrowing (Myers-Scotton, 1993, 2006). Cultural borrowing takes place to fill a gap in one's lexicon. In the early twentieth century, huge numbers of Western, mainly English-origin words entered the East Asian lexicon along with Western technology and ideas. However, this is no longer the case. Perhaps there is little need for foreign words in our lexicons because any gaps have already been filled by translated words. Despite this reduced need for cultural borrowing, the number of foreign words continues to increase because of core borrowing, in which foreign words enter another language not to fill a lexical gap, but to build a richer lexicon with which to communicate with the outside world. For example, the adoption of the term *coffee* reflects a cultural borrowing, filling a lexical gap within the English language. However, terms like *calamari* and *ojingeo* are core borrowings which do not fill a lexical gap, as these terms are already represented in English by the word *squid*, but offer lexical variety which can provide a richer meaning in context. The foreign-born words discussed in this book can be classified mostly as core borrowings.

However, the term *borrowing* has some inherent problems. As well as becoming more numerous, the identities and histories of imported words are becoming increasingly complex and diverse, and the terms traditionally used to refer to them, such as *borrowings* or *loanwords*, are no longer sufficient to describe their convoluted trajectories. As we shall discuss more from Chapter 3 onwards, one cannot label words with foreign heritage as loanwords simply because they are presented in romanised forms. Some locally made, second-generation English words have never been borrowed in the first place from so-called Inner Circle Englishes. In order to capture the diverse and complex histories of words born as a result of language contact between East Asian and English languages, I adopt the term *translingual words* in this book, following Kiaer (2019a).

1.2 Translingual words

Translingual is a term used to describe words with a complex life trajectory including identities, forms, and meanings that are hard to define based on the language ideology of a single nation-state. Translingual words cross language borders, constantly travelling and resettling in different languages. During their adaptation processes, they gain local forms and meanings, and therefore belong to multiple languages (Kiaer, 2019a). The notion of translingual words can also be linked to *translanguaging* – a concept defined as receiving information in one language, then using or applying it in a second language (Williams, 2002). Unlike code-switching, *translanguaging* does not require individuals to switch from one language to another, but rather allows a person to choose and assemble semiotic primitives sourced from their entire semiotic repertoire. In this way, the process of *translanguaging* disregards the imposed social and political boundaries between languages (García and Wei, 2014).

The concepts of transculturalism and transnationalism are important in understanding the nature of the translingual words that we discuss in this book. Transculturalism encompasses cultural encounters and their consequences for social identities and social, political, and economic structures. This concept highlights the three phases of cultural transmutation: acculturation, the transition of one culture into another; deculturation, a parallel process resulting in a loss of home culture; and transculturation, the creation of new cultural phenomena. Transnationalism can be defined as political, cultural, and economic processes which extend beyond nation-state boundaries.

In East Asia, regional tensions and colonialism have influenced transnational and transcultural trends. In recent years, East Asian countries have become increasingly interconnected through trade, migration, and popular culture. For example, transnationalism can be seen in the growth of Korean, Vietnamese, and Filipino diasporic communities in Japan; and transculturalism in the region is highly visible in international media industries, and exemplified by phenomena like *hallyu* (the Korean wave), cinema, and food culture (see Chapter 4).

Kiaer (2019a) argues that while languages are connected to certain linguistic environments, in today's world of increased migration and larger diasporic communities, languages can no longer be defined simply by their geographical information or nation-state identity. Lexical interaction between multiple languages produces shared words and new words for both languages. As lexical interaction progresses, the number of shared words increases, and these shared words start to be used separately in both language varieties. This dynamic lexical interaction becomes more complicated, producing complex hybridisations and creating new types of translingual words (Chapter 3).

1.3 Translingual words with new meanings, forms, and identities

As global interaction grows at an unprecedented rate, we are constantly exposed to new words with foreign origins, or from subcultures. As English establishes itself as a lingua franca (ELF) of our time, these words are mediated through, or at least represented globally in English by romanised forms. The ways in which these new words enter English are much more diverse than before. The development of social media and global branding in international trade are also contributing to a radical expansion of translingual food words (Chapters 4 and 5). In the past, these words entered English mainly through UK or US varieties, but nowadays they can enter English via various routes. Kiaer (2019a) showed that many East Asian-origin words entered World English through Southeast Asian varieties of English. Given the growth of linguistic and cultural contacts between East Asia and the English-speaking world, and the widespread use of English languages in daily life in the East Asian region, I predict that more and more hybrid English words featuring Asian-origin elements will begin to fill the lexicon of World Englishes (Chapter 3). Among these new words, food words show the most visible growth. This is due to the growth in exposure to local cuisines, but it is also related to the expansion of fusion cuisine across the world (Chapter 2). Social media and marketing strategies are also encouraging different, stylistic ways to represent food words (Chapters 4 and 5).

16 *Food words as translingual words*

In the social media era where ordinary people (as opposed to lexicographers) participate in word-making, we can observe how translation strategies differ based on individual translators' styles. For instance, translating for authenticity versus accessibility. There are various factors involved in such decisions: sometimes, words are transliterated deliberately to create a pun in the recipient language; or the choice of words may be dependent on the users' age. This book showcases diverse examples of East Asian food words used on Twitter. Users tend to be young people who are active on social media, and the way these words are presented may differ from how they are used in more traditional and formal writing. Normally, Twitter examples come with multi-modal resources such as photos and videos. It is therefore easy to understand what the word means in its local context. As we shall discuss in Chapter 4, Twitter and other social media spaces have also become important places where minority voices and their words can be captured, heard, and shared.

English as a lingua franca has also played the role of an intermediary word recipient for the rest of the world: romanised or Anglicised spellings and pronunciations often become popular and are then imported by other languages. Consider the following examples from Twitter which show how the phrase *sweet-and-sour* is used in different European languages such as German, French, Spanish, Portuguese, Dutch, and Italian (Figure 1.1).

Translingual words have meanings, forms, and identities that go beyond their language and culture of birth. First- and second-generation words, as well as global words, can gain the status of translingual words. Translingual words are used in all world languages, but will have romanised forms as well as their local forms. For instance, the word *sashimi* in the OED is defined as "a Japanese dish consisting of thin slices of raw fish served with grated radish or ginger and soy sauce", but nowadays the term *beef sashimi* is often used (Kiaer, 2019a: 60). Similarly, *bulgogi* in Korean refers to marinated and grilled meat, often beef or pork. Yet nowadays, the terms *tofu bulgogi* and *vegan bulgogi* are frequently found too (Figure 1.2).

The word *chilli* or *chili* is from Spanish. It originally comes from the name of a plant in the Central American Indian language in the sixteenth century. However, in the OED, *chilli sauce* is defined as a sauce made with tomatoes, peppers, and spices mainly found in the USA. The following quote can be found in the OED:

> 1846 A. M. Gilliam Trav. Mexico xi. 176 *I could eat no more, leaving my friend in full possession and enjoyment of his chili sauce.*

Food words as translingual words 17

Figure 1.1 Examples of 'sweet-and-sour' being used in different languages on Twitter.

Chilli powder is defined as a spice made from dried powdered red chillies. However, *chilli sauce* or *chilli powder* can now refer to various sauces, and their association with Asian cuisine is stronger than any other cuisine.

Similarly, *dumpling* and *noodle* were initially words that referred to food of British and German origin respectively, but nowadays they are used much more frequently in an Asian culinary context. According to

18 *Food words as translingual words*

Figure 1.2 Example of *vegan bulgogi* on Twitter.

Kiaer, Calway, and Ahn (ms), many British English speakers consider words like *dumpling* to be Pan-Asian or Chinese words, but they are also regarded as English words. Yet at the same time, diverse answers were found. Some even answered *dumpling* belongs to Caribbean cuisine (Chapter 2). Some words are used in a novel culinary context such as *Chinese tapas*, *rice burger*, or *sushi burrito* (Chapter 3). The process of romanisation inevitably changes the forms of East Asian-origin words. For example, *sake* in the OED was initially written as *saké*, with an accent as the following quote shows:

> 1947 J. Bertram *Shadow of War* 273 The guards looted the *saké* from their own stores.

Likewise for Vietnamese food words, the term *phở* is often simplified as *pho* and *bánh mì* is simplified as *bahn mi*. This simplification is understandable as it is not easy for the general public, the main users of these words, to remember and type relevant accents and tones (Chapter 4).

1.4 Entering English: transliterate/romanise or translate?

In this section, I show how Asian-origin words enter English. The strategies for this process have become greatly diversified. Sometimes words are romanised or transliterated, and other times they are translated. East Asian-origin food words have rapidly increased in English since the end of the nineteenth century. As we shall see in Chapter 2, most of these words are known to have Japanese or Chinese in origin, although there are a few keywords such as *soy*, *tofu*, or *hot pot* that are shared across East Asia.

Historically, since the beginning of the OED, lexicographers have viewed the growing number of foreign words primarily as assets, but they have sometimes been seen as a threat to English (Ogilvie, 2012). When words are considered a threat, it is easier to translate rather than transliterate them. This strategy is called *domestication* in translation theory, and is still popular today. However, foreign-origin words can be considered assets too, and can be introduced in their original forms through transliteration and romanisation. This is another common strategy known as *foreignisation* in translation theory. Venuti (1995) criticised the trend of erasing all traces of foreignness in translation as a form of ethnocentric violence, arguing that translators should deliberately foreignise their translations.

In China, until quite recently, English words entered Chinese through domestication – in translated forms – with only a few exceptions. However, as China's role in global trade has become increasingly essential, China's policy of translating all new vocabulary is now becoming much looser. The pressure to transliterate and romanise is rapidly growing, and now it is not hard to find Roman letters in shops in China.

When cultural awareness of a word is low, translated forms may be more common. Kiaer (2019a: 63) shows how distribution of the terms *soy sauce* and *shoyu* has changed: in earlier times *soy sauce* was preferred, but now *shoyu* is frequently found. Similarly, the term *miso soup* for the Japanese dish was predominant until 2000 but now, as Japanese culinary culture becomes more well known, *miso(-)shiru* also occasionally makes an appearance. In the past, when referring to East Asian varieties of hot pot, *soup* was invariably used as a translation for most cuisine. But now words like *pho* (Vietnamese), *jjigae* (Korean), and *shiru* (Japanese) are often used.

In the past, the routes by which words entered English depended on the linguistic authorities. As we shall see in Chapter 2, when foreign words entered local East Asian languages, they were often seen as 'English' words, and the forms and orthography were dictated by the national linguistic authorities. In the case of English, representative dictionaries such as the OED or major newspapers provided the guidelines for foreign-origin words. However, nowadays there are too many travelling words, many of whose etymological origins are not straightforward. The use of social media has opened a new avenue through which ordinary netizens can participate in the making and sharing of words. The ways in which netizens use words, such as social media orthography, can no longer be understood as marginal. The OED now even looks for textual evidence for new entries from Twitter.[2] Decisions about whether to foreignise or domesticate foreign-born words have become more difficult.

In terms of the existing translation theory, Skopos theory may be able to explain the ways in which foreign food words enter English. Skopos theory argues that the suitability of a translation is determined by its Skopos, meaning 'goal' (Nord, 2001). Skopos theory recognises translation as an 'act' which, like all acts, must have a goal. For example, a translation of Shakespeare's Hamlet into a Japanese manga comic with language which is easily understandable for children, and with certain adult themes removed, could be considered a good translation if the goal is to give young Japanese children an introduction to Shakespeare, even if the product is completely different from the source text. Kiaer (2019b) also proposes that the degree of domestication or foreignisation is at the translator's discretion.

Different methods co-exist in the adaption of most culinary terms. For cooking methods, words like *hot pot* or *stir-fry* are translated, but *yaki*, *char siu*, or *siu mei* are transliterated. Dumplings are another staple food in East Asia; though the word *dumpling* can be used in the Pan-Asian culinary context, transliterated local varieties such as *mandu* (Korean), *gyoza* (Japanese), *buuz* (Mongolian), and *jiaozi* (Chinese) are also popular.

Most of the first-generation food words that entered English in the early twentieth century are of Japanese or Chinese origin. Japanese words are mostly transliterated but for Chinese, many translated or calqued words are found. A calque is a special kind of translation whereby elements of an expression in the source language are translated literally into the target language. Examples of calque translations also include many food words. The term *sweet-and-sour* calqued from the Cantonese term 甜酸 (*tìhm syūn*) refers mainly to Chinese cuisine, which started appearing in the twentieth century, as shown in the following citation from the OED:

> 1932 L. GOLDING *Magnolia St.* v. 103 *Mrs. Emmanuel brought in some fish cooked in sweet-and-sour sauce.*

Terms for Sichuanese cuisine also include a number of calqued food words, such as *ants-climbing-a-tree*, *water-cooked meat*, *twice-cooked pork*, *tea-smoked duck*, and *hot-and-sour*. Interestingly, *sweet-and-sour* is in the OED, yet *hot-and-sour* is not, although both words show sufficient textual evidence.

Transliteration yields diverse forms, and the romanisation process is complicated. Korean *kochujang* – 'hot-pepper paste' – is a notable example. According to Google N-gram, which provides data up to 2000, the term *kochujang* is visible, but not the alternative spelling *gochujang*. However, *gochujang* is the term which appears in the OED, having been added quite recently in 2016. This may be because *gochujang* is the romanised form most popular on Twitter, and is also the transliterated form which follows the Revised Romanisation system proposed by the South Korean government. Between 2000 and 2010, the term *Korean pepper sauce* or *hot-pepper paste* were preferred to *gochujang* or *kochujang*. However, since the rise of the Korean wave and global awareness of Korean food, the Korean sauce has started to be known in its transliterated form *gochujang*. We can see from this example that the treatment of food words in English is also sensitive to time and space, as well as individual situations and speakers. For example, someone familiar with Korean cuisine may use the term *gochujang*, while a speaker who is less familiar with Korean cuisine and related terms, or who is speaking to an audience who is unfamiliar, may still prefer a translated term such as *hot-pepper paste*.

A common problem with transliteration or romanisation of East Asian languages is the issue of spacing. This is because some scripts, such as Chinese and Japanese, do not use spacing in their main script. Furthermore, even when an official system of romanisation has been adopted, it is often not used consistently. Inconsistencies in transliterated forms are exacerbated by competing systems of romanisation and individuals' creations of off-the-cuff transliterations, particularly on the internet. It is interesting to note the influence of computing technologies on the development and prevalence of romanised scripts; issues such as input methods become important considerations, and this can mean that more people gain access to the Roman alphabet through QWERTY keyboards. When the English language – or Roman alphabet – is more accessible, food names purely made in English are often created and used. This is particularly noticeable in Hong Kong and Macau. For instance, *pork chop*, *milk tea*, *pineapple cake*, and *egg tart* are locally made food words that were created in English and are popular in the region (Chapter 3).

1.5 Style matters

The idea of translingual words as it relates to individual expression goes hand in hand with Eckert's (2012) discussion of the 'third wave' of sociolinguistic theory, which examines how speakers intelligently juggle various styles to situate themselves where they want to be in the social landscape. Style in this sense not only refers to a certain mode of pronunciation or register of speech, but also includes word choice. That is, individual speakers choose words – beyond nation-state and perceived linguistic borders – to place themselves where they want to be in the given social landscape. As the number of words that successfully cross linguistic boundaries continues to increase, the use of words acquired from foreign sources will become less a matter of code-switching, and more a matter of assembling different styles to assert identity or convey information more efficiently and expressively in a given moment. In the following section, I introduce this theory with some examples of Japanese food words in English.

1.6 Case study: Japanese food words in English

As discussed above, when introducing an unfamiliar food item to Western audiences, two main strategies are employed: transliteration (romanisation) and translation. In romanisation, the Japanese word is simply converted into the Roman alphabet using an established system of correspondence with the Japanese syllabaries. An example using the Hepburn system of romanisation is *sashimi*, from the Japanese word 刺身 (*sashimi*, 'thinly sliced raw fish'). The term is normally not translated on British menus, but simply presented as 'sashimi' (Edamame, 2019b; Obento, 2019).

However, some words are typically not romanised on menus, but are translated instead. In some instances, a single word is chosen as the closest equivalent in the target culture. One example is the term 漬物 (*tsukemono*) which has been rendered as 'pickles' (Obento, 2019), despite the fact that the word 'pickle' in the UK generally refers to a kind of chutney sauce that is rather different in appearance and taste to Japanese *tsukemono*. Although the terms are not exactly equivalent, it is perhaps the closest match possible given the difference between Japanese and British food cultures: both food items are made using the core ingredients of vegetables and vinegar.

Alternatively, there are instances in which the Japanese term is calqued, a process also known as 'root-for-root translation'. In forming a calque, each morpheme of the original Japanese term is translated literally into English. A prime example is the Japanese dish 親子丼 (*oyakodon*), consisting of white rice topped with chicken and egg. The literal meaning of the term *oyakodon* is 'parent-and-child rice bowl', in reference to the use of both chicken and egg as ingredients. Accordingly, *oyakodon* has been translated in precisely this way in major British newspaper[3] *The Guardian*. Similarly, the term 手巻き (*temaki*), referring to rice with fillings inside a cone of dried seaweed, has been calqued as 'hand roll' (Tenshi, 2019b) (Figure 1.3).

Food words as translingual words 23

Figure 1.3 A bowl of 親子丼 (*oyakodon*, 'parent-and-child rice bowl').

A third strategy for translating unfamiliar food terms is to provide a short description of the item's appearance or ingredients. Common examples in a Japanese-British context are 小豆 (*azuki*), translated as 'red bean', and 鶏唐揚げ (*niwatori tōage*) which has been translated as 'Japanese fried chicken' (Japan Centre, 2019; YO! Sushi, 2019a).

The strategies of romanisation and translation can both have advantages for food retailers, depending on the context. When translating, the result is likely to be easier for a customer to pronounce than the original Japanese term. This may go some way towards explaining why a term like *tsukemono* is rendered as 'pickles' on British menus, as the original word is long and begins with 'ts' – an unusual combination for the start of an English-language word. Description of a food item's appearance can also be helpful for those customers who are unfamiliar with it. Even if someone has never been exposed to an *onigiri*, they will be able to visualise their order to some extent by knowing it is a 'type of rice ball' and feel reassured. Thus, translation may make a menu more accessible for customers who are not familiar with the Japanese language.

In contrast, among customers who are familiar with Japanese food, romanisation can help to aid rapid recognition of a food item. If an individual has previously seen 親子丼 (*oyakodon*) translated as 'chicken and egg rice', they may not recognise another menu's reference to 'parent-and-child rice bowl', even though both are plausible translations. However, if they are already familiar with the term *oyakodon*, then they will recognise the menu as serving something they have previously enjoyed. This is helped by the fact that major methods of romanising Japanese are not very divergent, and are therefore unlikely to hinder understanding in this particular example.

Finally, romanisation can be very useful for product marketing. In the section below, the usage of the word *yasai* in English is explored as a representative example.

1.6.1 Yasai and the exotic appeal of foreign words

Just because a word is romanised rather than translated, it does not mean there is not a close English semantic equivalent. For example, it is common in the UK to see the word 野菜 (*yasai*) transliterated from Japanese on menus, even though the word simply means 'vegetable' (Edamame, 2019a; Obento, 2019; Wagamama, 2019b). While the word 'vegetable' sounds ordinary, the word *yasai* sounds exciting. The transliteration of *yasai* is common, but by no means consistent in the case of Japanese-influenced restaurants in the UK. Indeed, the menu of popular 'pan-Asian' British restaurant chain *Wagamama* features both 'yasai gyoza' and 'vegetable tempura', despite the fact that 'vegetable gyoza' or 'yasai tempura' would also be valid (Wagamama, 2019b).

The word *yasai* has now been accepted into the English language as a fancy term for 'vegetable'. This is demonstrated by how the word is now used as a prefix even for dishes that are not Japanese in origin. The same Wagamama menu features 'yasai pad-thai', based on a Thai dish, and 'Yasai samla curry', based on Cambodian food (Wagamama, 2019a, 2019c). This illustrates how the use of the term *yasai* is motivated by marketing rather than faithfulness to the source language or culture (Chapter 5).

The appending of transliterated words like *yasai* to products that are not particularly related to the source culture is expanding. For instance, the British fast food chain Itsu sells '*zen* water' and chocolate '*oishi* bars' (lit. 'tasty bars') (Itsu, 2019b). These uses of Asian words are fairly redundant in terms of meaning, but are present to make the products appear 'exotic' and exciting, even if they are not actually related to Japanese culture.

1.6.2 Romanisation alongside translation

As discussed previously, there are advantages to both romanisation and translation in introducing Japanese food to a Western audience. In an attempt to reap the benefits of both methods, some Japanese food terms are half-translated and half-romanised by UK food outlets. A common example is the Japanese term 味噌汁, which is typically referred to on British menus as *miso soup*, whereas a full transliteration like *miso shiru* or a full translation like 'soybean paste soup' was not evidenced on the menus examined (Edamame, 2019a; Obento, 2019).

While '*miso* soup' is commonly served in the UK, the translation of food items that are still obscure to the vast majority of the population is a thornier issue. In these instances, the transliterated word alone will be unfamiliar. However, a description will convey a food item that the customer may never have eaten or even seen before, so may also be unhelpful. In such cases, both a transliteration and a description may be provided side by side. Examples from British menus include 'freshwater eel (*unagi*)' and '*yakisoba* (thin buckwheat noodles)' (Edamame, 2019b; Obento, 2019).

On some occasions, a transliteration is presented alongside a single word translation, rather than a multiword description. Typically, the English term is qualified by the Japanese word by prepending. This can have the unfortunate effect of duplicating meaning with strange results. To take one example, a popular British chain sushi restaurant sells '*kaiso* seaweed' (YO! Sushi, 2019b). Since the Japanese 海藻 (*kaisō*) is itself just a generic word for 'seaweed', the name of this product may appear somewhat odd to Japanese-English bilinguals, reading as 'seaweed seaweed'. Similarly, another major chain sells chocolate bars 'infused with *matcha* tea' (Itsu, 2019a). In Japanese, the morpheme 茶 (*cha*) in *matcha* means tea, with the effect that 'tea' appears twice in this phrase.

1.7 Summary

This chapter has introduced the concept of translingual words as words which cross language borders, constantly travelling and re-settling in different languages. Due to globalisation and migration patterns, and growing interest in global cuisines, culinary terms offer many rich examples of translingual words. Using food terms as an example, I have shown the various ways in which words enter the English language, and the impact this process can have on the forms, meanings, and identities of these words.

Notes

1 The term *mother tongue* is quite vague in the diverse, multilingual society we're living in. I have chosen to use the term birth language in this book.
2 Thanks to Dr Danica Salazar, World English Editor for the *Oxford English Dictionary*.
3 www.theguardian.com/lifeandstyle/2018/feb/08/six-of-the-best-rice-bowls-japanese-tim-anderson-nanban.

2 Early encounters
First-generation food words

This chapter presents various first-generation food words that entered English from East Asian languages. Many of the words from this region that have survived and thrived in English languages are culinary terms. Words from each region have followed different paths due to complex linguistic and cultural links with the English-speaking world. Though there are regional differences, most of these words entered English after 1850. Before mapping the routes these words took to enter the English language, I will briefly introduce the linguistic background of key languages in East Asia.

While the East Asian language situation is diverse and complex, many languages (Mongolian being a notable exception) share a history of interaction with Chinese characters and culture, and belong to the Chinese or Sino cultural sphere (汉字文化圈, *hànzì wénhuà quān*). Yet this term has its limitations. King (2015) proposes *sinographic cosmopolis* as an alternative concept to capture the linguistic and cultural reality of the region. Given that a large proportion of the words in this region are Sinitic common words (words shared in the Sinosphere), it is difficult to identify words as belonging to an individual nation-state language such as Korean, Japanese, or Chinese. This is because most of them share a great deal of traditional culture with each other. Approximately 50% of both Japanese and Korean words, at least those in the national dictionaries, are Sinitic-origin words (Kiaer, 2014; Shibatani, 1990) and historically the tradition of brush talk using Chinese script was the lingua franca between Japan and Korea too (Clements, 2019).

Without considering their Sinitic roots, it is impossible to delineate the linguistic and cultural identities of individual East Asian-origin words. As the influx of East Asian words into English increases, issues regarding the identity of Sinitic-origin words will also increase. It may be more accurate to label this group of words as Pan-East Asian or Sinitic-origin rather than country- or nation-specific (following

Kiaer, 2019a). In this text, I define Sinitic words as words which contain Chinese characters, either partially or totally. These words are not necessarily composed in a Chinese language context; most of the time, the assembly occurs in another linguistic context which has adopted Chinese characters as a part of its writing system, such as Japan or Korea. Likewise, Anglo words are words which contain English Roman letters, either partially or totally. They are not necessarily composed as words in a specifically English context, and their place of assembly can differ from their place of origin.

Most Pan-East Asian words found in East Asian culture are recorded in Western dictionaries as Chinese- or Japanese-origin words. For instance, *ganbei* (乾杯 *gānbēi*) which refers to a Chinese drinking toast literally meaning 'dry glass' is listed in the OED as a Chinese-origin word, yet Korean and Japanese both have the same Sinitic-origin word, albeit with different pronunciations. Though Sinitic heritages are shared, the history of language contact between each local language and European languages is shaped by individual nation-states' unique historical paths. Japan's interaction with the West was the most prominent and extensive, particularly with the English-speaking world. As a result, there are more words in the English language that come from Japanese than any other East Asian language.

2.1 The early influx of East Asian culinary terms into English

Historically, within interactions between East Asian and English languages, East Asian languages were more commonly recipients of new words from English than the other way around. There is evidence that scholars from China, Japan, and Korea collaborated in the process of receiving a great number of new words from English. No (2000) identified 5,466 new words introduced in the time of the Enlightenment period in Korea through translation. Among them, she found that 3,573 words (65.73%) are used in Korea, China, and Japan; 1,142 words (20.89%) are shared by Korea and Japan, but different in China; 271 words (4.96%) are shared by Korea and China, but different in Japan; and 480 (including 1 word shared in Chinese and Japanese) (8.78%) are different in all three countries. Examples shared by Korea, Japan, and China include words like 葡萄酒 'wine' or 科學者 'scientist'. Notably, the foreign, exotic food names that entered Korean or Japanese in the early twentieth century in transliterated forms – such as *coffee* and *banana* – are often regarded as English-sourced words, even though their origins lie elsewhere.

With the opening of East Asia to Western powers in the late nineteenth century, the English lexicon experienced an influx of East Asian terms. Although this was on a smaller scale than the linguistic borrowing from English into Asian languages, there was a clear trend of words making their way into English, many of which can be traced to the present day. The majority of Asian-origin terms in the English language originated from either Japanese or Chinese (Kiaer, 2019a). Japanese terms have been consistently entering the English language since contact began in the sixteenth century through trading and political missions, and the majority of terms that entered Western Englishes pertained to Japanese culture. Since the Meiji Restoration period of Westernisation and modernisation in the nineteenth century, contact with Japan has played a crucial role in introducing the first East Asian-origin words into English. Words like tofu, tsunami, and haiku were introduced during this period (Loveday, 1996). Most of these early words were, understandably, nouns, including a large number of culinary terms.

Chinese terms entering the English language have faced a chequered history, with political turmoil throughout the late nineteenth and twentieth centuries limiting the contact between the Chinese- and English-speaking worlds. However, almost as a direct product of this situation, the earliest terms imported into English were largely socio-politically distinctive words and culinary terms. The influx of terms from China is also diversified by the wealth of languages and dialects spoken in the region, which is especially noticeable when comparing English terms of either Mandarin or Cantonese origin. This has resulted in a wide variety of pronunciations, spellings, and translations occurring when Chinese terms are accepted into the English lexicon. While East Asian-origin terms relating to various topics have entered the English language, those which show the greatest staying power, surviving and thriving through the years, are cultural words, especially those describing food (Bolton, 2003).

Language contact yields new words for both contact languages. Kachru (1994) refers to this linguistic phenomenon as 'Englishisation', describing changes in the recipient language caused by language contact involving English. However, I challenge the idea of a passive 'recipient language', and note instead the ways in which both Englishised Asian words and Asian English words emerge as a result of language contact between Asian languages and English.

Durkin states that "it seems very unlikely that any of [these early origin words] were known to anything more than a very small circle of

English speakers" (Durkin, 2014: 396). However, as shown in Moody (1996), Yang Jian (2009), Zhong (2019), and, most recently, You, Kiaer, and Ahn (2019), the situation has changed.

Negative attitudes towards foreign words entering the English language have been noted. Take, for example, the following statement from 1973: "encroachment of alien words not only hinders understanding and solidarity among speakers, but also threatens the purity of a language by taking away its uniqueness and limiting its ability to create new words using its own linguistic sources" (Urquieta, 1973: 114; cited by Munoz–Basols and Salazar, 2016 and re-cited by You, Kiaer, and Ahn, 2019). Likewise, many East Asian linguistic authorities have proposed and conducted language purification movements, publishing monthly and yearly targets of foreign – mainly English – words which need to be replaced with local words. However, Adams (2017) shows that now even in North Korea, where any foreign-origin words have been strictly avoided, the prevalence of English words is nonetheless increasing due to the growth of English-language education.

In the following section, I shall show how the early settlers among food words from East Asian languages began their translingual journeys. This chapter discusses how first-generation food words from East Asian languages entered English, and how that influenced the (re)shaping of the meanings, forms, and identities of those words. I begin by introducing various language situations in East Asia, and providing examples from each region. I then show how these words are used in different varieties of English: UK, US, and Australian, as well as Singaporean and Hong Kong Englishes. I present examples from diverse sources, both offline and online, incorporating mass and social media. I also demonstrate how word users' attitudes towards first settler words have changed, and how English grammar is coping with first-generation food words.

2.2 Language situations in East Asia

Language situations in East Asia are complex and diverse. Different languages' routes of Westernisation and the ways in which their vocabulary has settled into English vary greatly. Alongside this variation, in recent years transcultural and transnational trends have impacted the whole region. This is particularly visible in the uses of culinary terms. Below I give a brief introduction to the different regional languages that are dealt with in this text, and comment on their historical interaction with English and the Roman alphabet.

2.2.1 Mainland China

The official language in the PRC is Modern Standard Mandarin – although various other languages including Tibetan, Mongolian, and Uyghur are recognised as regional languages – and there are numerous dialects spoken. Modern Mandarin is written using simplified Chinese characters. Mandarin has many English-origin words, such as 'brownie' (布朗尼 *bùlángní*); uses Roman letters and English abbreviations, for example *APP* ('mobile application'); and has a small number of words which integrate Roman letters and Chinese characters, such as 'T-shirt' (T恤 *T xù*).

The official system of romanisation is Hanyu Pinyin, adopted by the PRC in 1979. This is the system I employ in this book. The Wade-Giles system is commonly seen in older academic texts or references to them. Hanyu Pinyin is used on a daily basis by native Chinese speakers to type on computers and smartphones. However, there are still methods which allow direct input of handwritten Chinese characters using trackpads. Indication of tones has posed a problem in the romanisation of Mandarin; they can be indicated through accents above letters, or numbers after individual morphemes. In some systems, tones are omitted entirely. The standard nowadays is for tones to be indicated using accents, for example: *nǐhǎo* (你好, 'hello').

2.2.2 Hong Kong and Macau

The official languages of Hong Kong are Chinese and English, and regionally the type of Chinese spoken is Cantonese. The official languages of Macau are Chinese and Portuguese, with Cantonese spoken as the local variation of Chinese. Cantonese is written using traditional Chinese characters, with the addition of some special characters not present in Mandarin. Because Hong Kong was under British colonial rule until 1997, Hong Kong Cantonese adopted a lot of English-origin words, some of which then travelled to the mainland. This is why some English-origin words in Mandarin sound very different from the original English word – because the process of transliteration went through Cantonese first.

There are a number of different romanisation systems for Cantonese. The Hong Kong Government Cantonese Romanisation is used in naming streets and so on, but is unpublished. It is based on the Standard Romanisation system. Cantonese Pinyin is the system accepted by the Hong Kong Examinations and Assessments Authority. Yale romanisation of Cantonese is also widely used, and is the system used in this book. Cantonese is primarily a spoken language, which has posed problems in the standardisation of its written forms.

2.2.3 Taiwan

Mandarin Chinese is used in schools and for business, and Hokkien and Hakka are also prevalent. There are also Formosan and other minority languages spoken by Taiwanese indigenous peoples. Taiwan uses Bopomofo as a system for transliterating Taiwanese Mandarin using phonetic symbols. There are also Bopomofo keyboards which enable the typing of Chinese characters without the use of Roman letters. Hanyu Pinyin was adopted as the official standard for romanisation in 2009, but Bopomofo is still widely in use. Hokkien can be written in Chinese characters with some special character additions. From the nineteenth century, Hokkien has also been written using *Pe̍h-ōe-jī*, the first Romanised writing system for Taiwanese Hokkien, which was later adapted into the Taiwanese Romanisation System, the officially promoted romanisation of Hokkien since 2006.

2.2.4 Tibet

Standard Tibetan is spoken on the Tibetan plateau and in parts of Nepal. The written language is based on Classical Tibetan and written with an Indic script. The Wylie transliteration system is most commonly used by scholars to render Tibetan into the Latin alphabet. However, the official romanisation system accepted by the PRC is Tibetan Pinyin. Most secondary schools teach in Mandarin Chinese; however, monolingual Tibetan teaching is common in early education. There are approximately 40 English-origin words in modern Tibetan (Hsieh and Kenstowicz, 2008).

2.2.5 Japan

The official language is Japanese, in which there are a large number of English-origin words. Modern Japanese is written using a combination of characters originating from Chinese (*kanji*) and native Japanese syllabaries (*hiragana* and *katakana*). There are three main systems of romanisation, and the Hepburn system is the most widely used. Almost all Japanese speakers are able to read and write romanised Japanese, although it is rarely used. During the Meiji era, there was talk of abolishing the Japanese writing system altogether in favour of using *romaji* (romanised Japanese), but this was never adopted. Japanese is written without spacing, so there is difficulty in knowing where to input spaces in romanised scripts. Long vowels also pose a problem; accents are used to indicate long vowels but are often omitted in practice.

2.2.6 South Korea

The official language is Korean, and there are several systems of romanisation. The two most common are Revised Romanisation of Korean, which is the officially adopted method of romanisation and the method used in this book, and the McCune-Reischauer system, which is often found in older academic texts. Modern Korean is written using Hangul. Korean has many English-origin words, which Hangul is capable of transliterating into Korean with very little change in pronunciation. One issue in the romanisation of Korean is the representation of consonants which do not exist in English. Furthermore, although there is an official romanisation system, it is not used consistently by all those engaging with the Korean language. This – in addition to dialect differences – has led to discrepancies such as the surname '이' being romanised in many different ways including Lee, Yi, I, and Rhee.

2.2.7 North Korea

The official language is Korean. North Korea officially uses the Romanisation of Korean system, which replaced the McCune-Reischauer system in 1992. In contrast to the prevalence of English-origin words in South Korea, the North Korean language has far fewer English-origin words due to a government drive to resist foreign terms. The foreign-origin words that do exist in North Korea tend to derive from Japanese or Russian.

2.2.8 Mongolia

The official language is Mongolian, and the official writing system uses a Cyrillic alphabet which is identical to the Russian alphabet except for the addition of two extra letters. The Roman alphabet was adopted for Mongolian for a brief period, but was quickly replaced by the Cyrillic alphabet, supposedly for political reasons. The romanisation of Mongolian Cyrillic uses the BGN/PCGN 1964 System.[1] There are very few English-origin words in Mongolian.

2.2.9 Vietnam

The national language is Vietnamese, which was originally represented in writing using Classical Chinese. Literary works used Classical Chinese with additional characters to represent native Vietnamese words. At the end of the nineteenth and early twentieth centuries,

First-generation food words 33

there was a gradual adoption of the Roman alphabet (*chữ Quốc ngữ*). Its use was eventually made mandatory under French colonisation in 1910, and it is now the only writing system taught, although Chinese characters are still studied by some and used for calligraphy. There are a moderate number of English-origin words in Vietnamese.

2.3 East Asian food words in the OED

The OED advanced search identifies 80 food words in English which are of East Asian origin. Currently, there are 27 words of Chinese origin, 42 words of Japanese origin, 5 words of Korean origin, 3 words of Tibetan origin, and 3 words of Vietnamese origin. In this search, 'food words' means words referring to a dish, drink, or other element of culinary culture, including kitchen utensils, equipment, and ingredients. While verbs, adjectives, and adverbs would also have been classified as food words, all the entries mentioned in the OED advanced search are nouns.

Words such as *stir-fry* or *sweet-and-sour* do not show any East Asian heritage, though it is mentioned that these words are usually used in Chinese cooking. In the case of *stir-fry*, the OED notes that it is mainly used in the USA. Most of these words entered English in the twentieth century, particularly between 1900 and 1980. However, the earliest quote for East Asian cuisine is found in 1616, for the Japanese noun *miso*. The most recent quote was in 1985, featuring the Vietnamese noun *banh mi*. The year when the quotes are found is different from the year when these words entered the OED. While the words listed are considered the standardised spellings in English, restaurants and shops may use a different spelling (Chapter 5).

The words below are categorised according to etymology and the year when the first quote appeared according to the OED. It is worth noting that a number of words have experienced contact with other languages before entering English, so it can be slightly difficult to distinguish the exact root, as in the case of *soy* and *tofu*.

2.3.1 China

bao (1971), *baozi* (1927), *char kway teow* (1973),[2] *chop suey* (1888), *chow mein* (1903), *choy sum* (1939), *fu yung* (1917), *hoisin* (1957), *jiaozi* (1978), *ketchup* (1682),[3] *li* (1945), *li ting* (1958), *Mao-tai* (1962), *mien* (1890), *moo goo gai pan* (1902), *moo shu* (1962), *seitan* (1968), *shumai* (1951), *siu mei* (1960), *soy* (1696), *subgum* (1902), *Szechuan* (1945), *tofu* (1880), *Twankay* (1840), *wok* (1952), *won ton* (1948), *yuan hsiao* (1945).

2.3.2 Japan

dashi (1963), *edamame* (1951), *gobo* (1822), *gyoza* (1965), *kaiseki* (1920), *maguro* (1880), *maki zushi* (1914), *matcha* (1881), *Midori* (1978), *mirin* (1874), *miso* (1615), *mizutaki* (1933), *mochi* (1616), *natto* (1899), *nori* (1891), *omakase* (1979), *omochi* (1899), *panko* (1970), *ponzu* (1966), *ramen* (1962), *saké* (1687),[4] *sashimi* (1880), *shabu-shabu* (1970), *shiso* (1873), *shochu* (1938), *soba* (1896), *suimono* (1890), *sukiyaki* (1920), *sunomono* (1900), *sushi* (1893), *tataki* (1971), *tempura* (1920), *teppan-yaki* (1970),[5] *teriyaki* (1961), *toro* (1971), *udon* (1920), *umami* (1963), *umeboshi* (1822), *wakamame* (1950), *yakisoba* (1957), *yakitori* (1962), *yokan* (1875).

2.3.3 Korea

bibimbap (1977), *doenjang* (1966), *gochujang* (1966), *makkoli* (1970), *soju* (1951).

2.3.4 Tibet

chang (1800), *momo* (1922), *tsampa* (1852).

2.3.5 Vietnam

banh mi (1985), *chao tom* (1969), *nuoc mam* (1885).

The distribution of East Asian words is different in other Englishes. For instance, Merriam-Webster includes words not found in the OED, such as *bulgogi*. Compared to US or UK Englishes, Australian English appears to contain a wider variety of Asian-origin food words. For instance, the Macquarie dictionary features the following words all including '*yaki*': *yaki nori, yakisoba, okonomiyaki, sukiyaki, teppanyaki*, and *teriyaki*. Words such as *okonomiyaki* are only found in the Macquarie dictionary (*okonomiyaki* is defined as a Japanese savoury pancake with a variety of ingredients in the batter, toppings, and a thick, sweet sauce).

2.4 The Duden case: selection criteria for new words in German

In the case of the OED or other English dictionaries, lexicographers look for written evidence to justify the inclusion of new terms, gathering data from various texts including literary and non-literary journals, databases, newspapers, and even social media. However, there are no clear guidelines on which words to include in English dictionaries. Unlike English, German has a clear set of rules. Below, I show how words are selected and included in the German dictionary Duden.[6]

Unlike the OED, selection criteria for foreign words entering the Duden are explicitly documented. No words are ever taken out of the OED, but obsolete words are removed from the Duden. According to the introductory video on how words enter the Duden (2012), the process is as follows: a large software database continually follows published texts (newspapers, magazines, books, and so on) and tests individual words for how widespread they are, how often they are used, and how sustained the usage is. If a word appears often enough, it enters the Duden, but if it's not a clear-cut case, it is discussed by a team who then decide whether to include it or not.

The Goethe-Institut (2011) specifies that the Duden database looks at texts from Germany, Austria, and Switzerland. Only words established in common language come into the Duden, so they have to appear in a wide variety of different texts. A words must occur more than 50 times to qualify. In this way, they hope to avoid words only popular for a short while, or those which only appear in certain specialised literature.

The Duden has been rather controversial with regard to its attitude towards foreign words; critics claim that the Duden accepts foreign words indiscriminately. However, editors have responded that they are simply reflecting what happens in language, and the Duden's staff mission statement says: "we document the usage of a word; we are not a dictionary of the pure German language". The Duden also gives guidelines on how to make foreign words fit into German, such as how to conjugate new verbs. In addition, Duden has published a 'dictionary of scene language' – that is, a dictionary which follows trends much more closely, and hence includes many more foreign words.

2.5 Forms of first-generation translingual words

When words enter a new language, there are not always set conventions on how this transition should happen, or what form the words should take in the new language. Nevertheless, most words that belong to the first generation of translingual words which entered the English lexicon in the early twentieth century show little variation in terms of their forms and orthographic variation. For instance, 김치 is spelt consistently as *kimchi*, rather than *gimchi* or *kimchee*, which appear rarely. However, the first-generation words that entered English in recent years show greater variation in terms of their forms and romanisation. For instance, *kimbap*, which has the same initial consonant property as *kimchi*, is known mostly as *gimbap*, *kimbap*, or *Korean sushi*. Among these, *gimbap* is the most popular spelling and is found in the Macquarie dictionary. *Kalbi*, referring to Korean BBQ, was more popular than *galbi* until the year 2000, according to Google N-gram. But now, *galbi* is more frequently seen than *kalbi*, though both are used in World Englishes.

Words like *Peking duck* are also worth mentioning. This phrase is the direct calqued translation of 北京烤鸭 (*Běijīng kǎoyā*). Since the mid-1980s, 北京 (*Běijīng*) has been primarily transliterated as *Beijing* rather than *Peking*. Prior to this shift, the term *Peking duck* was preferred to *Beijing duck* (Figure 2.1).

Most first-generation food words are expressed in transliterated forms. However, occasionally there are translated or calqued forms. Another example is *chopstick*, which entered the OED in 1889. The Chinese term for chopsticks – 筷子 *kuàizi* – contains a character with the exact same sound value as the word 快 *kuài* meaning 'quick'. 'Chop' or 'chop chop' is a pigeon-English term meaning 'quick' or 'quickly' potentially derived from the Cantonese 速速 *chūk chūk*. Through this complex pathway, 筷子 *kuàizi* became 'chopsticks'. The first quote in the OED is found in 1699 as below:

> 1699 W. DAMPIER *Voy. & Descr.* I. iv. 85 At their ordinary eating… they use two small round sticks about the length and bigness of a Tobacco-pipe. They hold them both in the right hand, one between the fore-finger and thumb; the other between the middle-finger and the fore-finger… They are called by the English Seamen Chopsticks.

Words like *chopstick* have entered other European languages in their calqued forms. These words lose their foreignness relatively quickly.

In most cases, items like *sushi, karaoke, samurai,* and *kimchi* are pronounced according to local accent patterns. In other words, their Roman alphabet transliteration is pronounced naturally as a French, German, or Italian speaker would, and so on. So, while the spelling is universal, pronunciation follows local patterns, and the result is much closer to the Japanese pronunciation in some cases than in others. When it comes to Chinese food terms such as *sweet and sour* and *Peking duck*, they were often represented in local translation, for example *aigre-douce* and *canard de Pékin*, respectively, in French.

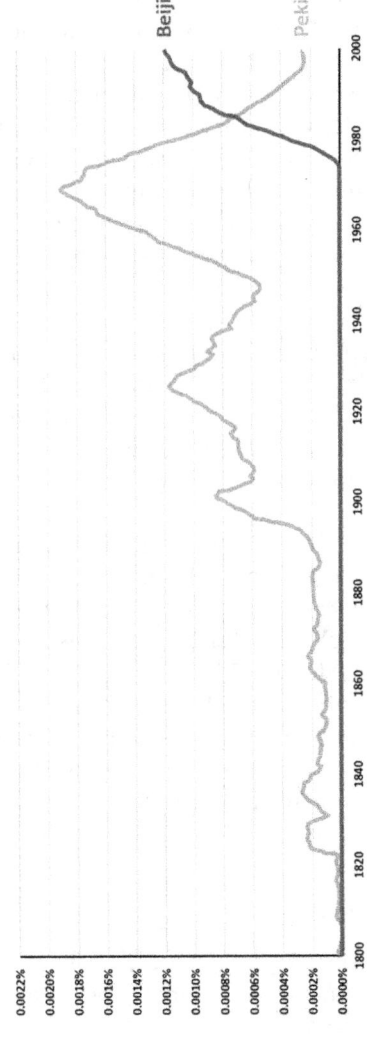

Figure 2.1 Graph showing transition from use of Peking to Beijing, 1800–2000.

2.6 Meanings of first-generation translingual words

2.6.1 Sushi and Peking duck

You, Kiaer, and Ahn (2019) have published the results of interviews with British university students about their understanding of East Asian-origin words. Though the students were very familiar with words like *sushi* or *kimchi*, the survey found that their understanding of what the word *sushi* referred to varied. Opinion was divided as to whether *sushi* referred to a way of preparing rice with vinegar, raw fish, or to a dish involving rice with fish or other ingredients.

Similarly, *Peking duck* in the Macquarie dictionary is defined as "a dish consisting of small pancakes wrapped around pieces of crisp roast duck skin with spring onions, cucumber, and hoisin sauce, the flesh of the duck being traditionally served separately". However, the OED defines it as

> a Chinese dish consisting of strips of roast duck served with shredded vegetables and a sweet sauce. Merriam-Webster defines *Peking duck* as a Chinese dish consisting of roasted duck meat and strips of crispy duck skin topped with scallions and sauce and wrapped in thin pancakes.

As we can see, the three definitions are all slightly different. The term *Peking duck* is used more frequently in Australian or Hong Kong English than in US or UK varieties. According to the corpus of Global Web-Based English (GloWbE), *Peking duck* has a per mille value of 0.51 in Australian English, and 2.27 in Hong Kong English, whereas it has a per mille value of 0.04 in UK English, and 0.08 in US English. The per mille value refers to parts-per-thousand, and can be used to compare proportionally how often a word is used in a given country or population. This value makes for clearer comparison between countries than the number of usages.

2.6.2 Noodle and dumpling

According to the OED, the word 'noodle' was originally borrowed from the German language term *Nudel*. The term *Nudel* was itself probably a variant of the word *Knödel*, a type of German dumpling. The term *Knödel* is still applied in German cooking, but refers to a rather different food product that is not string-like. Despite the word's German origin, it is now commonly used to refer to the wheat flour noodles that are heavily represented in the traditional cuisines of Asian countries like Korea, Japan, and Vietnam.

First-generation food words 39

The word *dumpling* is also a European-origin term that was subsequently applied to Asian cooking. *Dumpling*, as an umbrella term, can include a range of food items like *baozi, jiaozi, gyoza, mandu, manti, momo,* and *ravioli*. The term was previously established as referring to suet dumplings or Scottish clootie dumplings, but has gained an almost entirely new connotation in modern English in reference to Asian dumplings.

2.7 Identities of first-generation translingual words

Some first-generation words re-enter the language of departure. There are instances where words have initially been borrowed from English into Asian languages, and later 'reborrowed' back into English, such as in the case of Euro-Japanese nineteenth-century *yōshoku* words. *Yōshoku* is the Japanese term for Western foods, which first entered Japanese food culture during the Meiji Restoration (Kiaer, 2019a). Now, some of these words have returned to English again from Japanese. These can be referred to as 'boomerang words'. For example, *beer* was a first-generation English word that settled in Japanese. Now, the Japanised form of *beer*, namely *beeru*, has started to be used in English, as found in the Twitter example below (Figure 2.2).

Katsu is another so-called 'boomerang word'. *Katsu* is originally from the English word 'cutlet' that travelled into Japanese, but the term has now been imported back into English to refer to deep fried cutlets, as used in Japanese cooking. *Katsu* is now used to refer to a specifically Japanese-style cutlet dish, and it is frequently used in English and other languages. The following Twitter examples show how *katsu* is used in French (Figure 2.3).

Figure 2.2 Boomerang word *beeru* on Twitter.

Figure 2.3 Boomerang word *katsu* on Twitter.

Many compounds with *katsu* are found. For instance, references to pork cutlet as *ton katsu, don katsu, pork katsu,* or *katsu don*.

Consider, also, the word *tempura*. *Tempura* is a dish consisting of prawn, shrimp, white fish, or vegetables, coated in a light batter and deep-fried. The word *tempura*, referring to the food item or the technique of dipping fish and vegetables into a batter and frying them, comes from the word 'tempora', a Latin word meaning 'times' or 'time period', which was used by both Spanish and Portuguese missionaries to refer to the Lenten period or Ember Days refer to holy days when Catholics avoid red meat and instead eat fish or vegetables. The term *tempura* is thought to have first gained popularity in southern Japan; it became widely used to refer to any sort of food prepared using hot oil, including some already existing Japanese foods. Today, the word *tempura* is also commonly used to refer to *satsuma-age*, a fried fish cake which is made without batter.

Generally, translingual food words that entered into the English lexicon have become nativised into English, and people consider these words at least as dual identity words, if not entirely English terms. Many European culinary terms which enter the English lexicon lose their foreignness more quickly and easily than those of East Asian origin. For instance, people now consider *sushi* familiar enough to be an English word but they will remember its Japanese heritage. By contrast, European-origin words such as *coffee* or *mocha* are not thought of as foreign words.

Compared to other European languages, the German dictionary Duden contains significantly more East Asian-origin words. The following words of East Asian origin in the Duden were not found in French, Spanish, or Portuguese dictionaries. B refers to the words that entered into German earlier than the twentieth century, and N, M, and F refer to genders (Table 2.1).

Table 2.1 East Asian-origin words in the Duden

chanoyu	BN	Tea ceremony as Japanese custom
chawan	BM	Tea bowl used during Japanese tea ceremony
edamame	BF	Japanese dish of salted green soybeans boiled in their pods
fugu	BN	Pufferfish that is eaten as a Japanese delicacy
kaki	BF	Japanese persimmon
kombucha	BM	Tea fungus, tea fermented with kombucha
mutsu	BM	Kind of apple
shiitake	BM	Leaf mushroom with reddish brown cap and firm whiteish flesh

2.8 Case study: romanising Japanese menus

This section looks at first-generation Japanese words found in British menus. As mentioned in Chapter 1, there is a range of different methods used in introducing Japanese food terms to a Western audience. These fall into the two broad categories of romanisation and translation. Based on an analysis of online menus of Japanese-influenced restaurants in the UK, translation methods included: selection of a single word that is the closest English semantic equivalent, calquing, and multiple word description. Sometimes, romanised terms were presented alongside a translation. Among the romanised terms on menus, omitting the representation of long vowels was a common feature. Similarly, there is a tendency to present the English spelling of borrowed Japanese words that have English cognates.

2.8.1 Romanisation of chō'on ('long sounds')

The Japanese language in its standard form distinguishes between short and long vowels. In the commonly used Hepburn system of romanisation, long vowels are represented either by placing a macron above the letter (*tō*), or by letter duplication (*too*). In the English menus studied, I found some instances of letter duplication to reflect long vowels. For instance, 椎茸 (*shītake*), a type of East Asian mushroom, was written 'shiitake' (Tenshi, 2019a). However, it was much more common to ignore the long vowel altogether, with the word presented as if it contained a short vowel instead. The numerous examples include 海藻 (*kaisō*, 'seaweed') spelled as 'kaiso', カレー (*karē*, 'curry') spelled as 'kare', and ラーメン (*rāmen*, 'noodles in soup') spelled as 'ramen' (Obento, 2019; Tenshi, 2019a; YO! Sushi, 2019b). It is not clear why these long vowels are not represented. One explanation is that the macron diacritic is not typically used in English, so it may confuse customers. Letter duplication could also mislead people in their pronunciation if they are not familiar with Japanese romanisation methods. The letter sequence 'oo', for example, is commonly used to represent /uː/ in English rather than /oː/.

2.8.2 Romanisation of gairaigo ('loanwords')

Japanese contains a very large number of foreign-origin words. The most common source language for these words is Chinese, although Japanese has also borrowed from other Asian languages like Korean and Ainu (Shibatani, 1990). Since the 1600s, contact with Westerners has led to the Japanese language adopting lexical items from many European languages, including Dutch, Portuguese, and, most prominently, English. These borrowings are referred to in Japanese as 外来語 (*gairaigo*), literally meaning 'words from outside'. *Gairaigo* are often written using the *katakana* syllabic script in modern Japanese. Some prominent examples of food-related *gairaigo* from English include: トマト (*tomato*, 'tomato'), ケーキ (*kēki*, 'cake'), and ホットドッグ (*hotto doggu*, 'hot dog').

As is clear from cases such as *hotto doggu*, words are assimilated to the Japanese sound system as part of the borrowing process. As a result, Japanese *gairaigo* that originate in English are not necessarily comprehensible to English native speakers. An additional obstacle to the understanding of *gairaigo* by English speakers is the phenomenon of 和製英語 (*wasei eigo*), terms coined inside Japan using borrowed English elements. An example from the food world is オムライス (*omuraisu*), referring to a Japanese dish of omelette with fried rice and ketchup. The term is a portmanteau of the English-origin words オムレツ (*omuretsu*, 'omelette') and ライス (*raisu*, 'rice'). Although *omuraisu* is considered *gairaigo* because it is composed entirely of borrowed English elements, generally only English speakers who have spent time in Japan are familiar with the term.

2.8.3 English-derived terms

When representing *gairaigo* originally derived from English, there are two main options: romanise the form that has been assimilated to the Japanese sound system as if it were any other Japanese word, or use the original English spelling. For example, ケーキ (*kēki*, 'cake') could be rendered either as 'kēki', reflecting the Japanese pronunciation, or simply as 'cake', reflecting the original English. In the menus, there were multiple examples of English *gairaigo* romanisation reflecting the Japanese assimilated form. To illustrate, ライスカレー (*raisukarē*, 'curry with rice') was rendered as 'raisukaree' by one restaurant chain, despite the word consisting of the English components ライス (*raisu*, 'rice') and カレー (*karē*, 'curry') (Wagamama, 2019a). Similarly, バターほうれん草 (*batā hōrensō*, 'buttered spinach') was listed in a different menu as 'bata horenso' although バター (*batā*) is a borrowing from the English word 'butter' (Edamame, 2019a).

In the case of *wasei eigo* words, the English terms coined inside Japan, the assimilated Japanese form was usually romanised. One example is サーモンフライ (*sāmon furai*), referring to deep fried salmon fillet, which was romanised as *samon furai* (Edamame, 2019a). The component サーモン (*sāmon*) is from English 'salmon' and フライ (*furai*) is from the English verb 'to fry'. However, there were also instances where *wasei eigo* components were rendered with the original English spelling. Notably, カツカレー (*katsu karē*) was rendered as *katsu curry* on multiple menus, reflecting the English origin of the term *karē* (Obento, 2019; Wagamama, 2019a). 'Katsu curry' is therefore a hybrid, where the first component of the transliterated *wasei eigo* term reflects the assimilated Japanese form and the latter component reflects the English source word (see Chapter 3 for more examples). This illustrates the lack of any hard and fast rule for whether the Japanese or English spelling will be used in the transliteration of English *gairaigo* words.

2.8.4 Terms derived from third languages

As with English *gairaigo* terms, it appears there is no consistent rule for how British restaurants romanise terms derived from source languages other than English. In the case of third language terms, such as borrowings from Korean, either the source language term will be romanised or the Japanese assimilated version will be romanised, but the selection of method is unpredictable. For example, the Japanese term キムチ (*kimuchi*) refers to a type of side dish made from vegetables. The word is from Korean 김치 *kimchi* which also refers to a side dish made from fermented and salted vegetables – a staple of the country's traditional cuisine. Japanese kimuchi tends to be sweeter than the spicy Korean kimchi. The romanised form *kimchi*, reflecting the original Korean pronunciation of the word, was found on one British Japanese restaurant menu (Obento, 2019). However, the spelling *kimuchi*, reflecting the Japanese pronunciation, was found on another (Edamame, 2019b).

In other cases, the Japanese assimilated form was consistently romanised. For example, 餃子 (*gyōza*, 'fried dumpling'), which comes from the Chinese, 饺子 (*jiǎozi*) in Mandarin, was consistently romanised as 'gyoza' on menus (Tenshi, 2019a; Wagamama, 2019b). Interestingly, one restaurant romanised 炒飯 (*chāhan*), borrowed from the Chinese 炒饭 (*chǎofàn*), as *cha fan*, halfway between the Chinese and Japanese pronunciations (Obento, 2019). It is not clear whether this was intentional.

For European languages genetically affiliated with English, there is an additional option with regard to food terms that have English cognates. Specifically, the English spelling may be presented instead of a romanised form of Japanese or the spelling used in the original source language. For example, it has been argued that the Japanese word サラダ (*sarada*, 'salad') is borrowed from Portuguese, where the equivalent word is *salada*. On menus, the romanisation *sarada* was detected, but there were no instances of the Portuguese *salada* (Edamame, 2019a). The English cognate *salad*, however, was often substituted. For example, ゴマワカメサラダ (*goma wakame sarada*), a dish of marinated seaweed with sesame seeds, was presented as *goma wakame salad* (Tenshi, 2019a).

2.9 Case studies: first-generation food words

Each food word carries its own history of cultural interaction. In the following section, I discuss examples of first-generation food words of East Asian origin and their translingual properties.

2.9.1 *Momo*

Momo is a Tibetan-origin word. In the OED, it is defined as a word used in Tibetan cookery, usually in the plural, to refer to a type of dumpling:

> Usually in *plural*. In Tibetan cookery: a steamed dumpling filled with meat (or occasionally vegetables).
>   1922 *Amer. Church Monthly* Mar. 592 I did up 70 packages in red paper containing a momo, or dumpling, two little cakes, a cup of peanuts and six pieces of clear candy.
>   1989 *Passport* Aug.–Sept. 20/3 We…celebrated the completion of the trek with copious draughts of tea and piles of steamed momos (meat dumplings).
>   1998 P. CHAPMAN *1999 Good Curry Guide* 133 Nepalese food is very different and must be sampled. Momos (spicy dumpling) are highly recommended as are all the dishes.

2.9.2 Chang

This is another word from Tibetan. It refers to the name of a type of beer typically made from barley, rice, or millet. Consider these quotes from the OED:

> 1800 S. TURNER *Acct. Embassy Court Teshoo Lama* I. ii. 24 Chong is a slightly acid and spirituous liquor.
> 1887 *Field* 19 Feb. 243/1 The headman came out with jugs of 'chang' (a kind of beer made from grass).

2.9.3 Tsamba

In Tibet, it is a staple food made from barley meal. The following example is from Twitter (Figure 2.4).

2.9.4 Moon cake

In the OED, *moon cake* is defined as a round cake traditionally eaten during Chinese mid-autumn festivities. It is calqued directly from the Chinese term 月饼 (*yuèbǐng*: *yuè*, 'moon'; *bǐng*, 'cake'). In the OED, the first written quote is found in 1688:

> 1688 tr. G. de Magalhães *New Hist. China* xx. 318 The preceding Days they send to one another Presents of little Loaves and Sugar-Cakes, which they call *Yue Pim*, or Moon-Cakes. They are round,.. and represent the Full Moon.

In the Macquarie, this word is defined as a type of small Chinese cake with a filling of sweet bean paste.

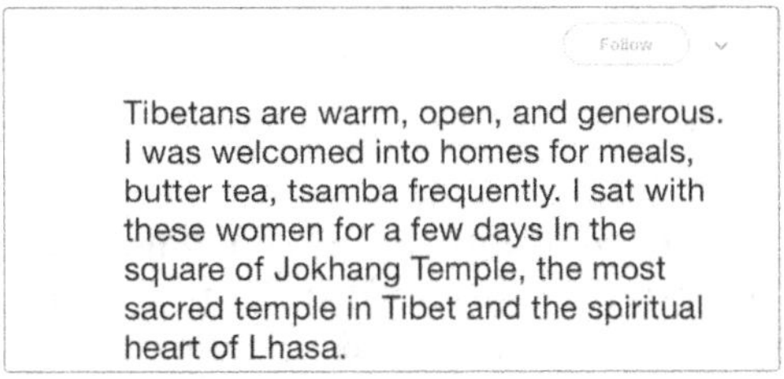

> Tibetans are warm, open, and generous. I was welcomed into homes for meals, butter tea, tsamba frequently. I sat with these women for a few days In the square of Jokhang Temple, the most sacred temple in Tibet and the spiritual heart of Lhasa.

Figure 2.4 Tsamba on Twitter.

2.9.5 Spring roll

Spring roll is another calqued first-generation food word. In the OED, it is defined as a word used in Chinese cookery which refers to a small pancake or similar base filled with vegetables (and sometimes also meat), rolled into a cylinder, and deep-fried. It is a direct calque from the Chinese word 春卷 (*chūnjuǎn: chūn*, 'spring', with connotations of newness and freshness; *juǎn*, 'to roll'), probably originally named because vegetable snacks were associated with the spring festival. Interestingly, the Macquarie includes the phrases 'Vietnamese spring roll' and 'Vietnamese mint'. The strong Vietnamese influence in Australia may be the reason why more Vietnamese cultural items can be found in the Macquarie.

2.9.6 Sencha and matcha

Sencha is a type of Japanese tea made from green tea leaves that have been steamed, rolled, and dried. It is known as a Japanese borrowing – but the original words that make up *sencha* are from Middle Chinese. This word, together with many tea-related words, is understood as Japanese-origin words despite their Chinese heritage.

> 1867 J. C. HEPBURN *Japanese & Eng. Dict.* 389/2 Sen-cha... Infusion of tea-leaves.

Matcha shows the same translingual journey. *Mat* is from *matsu* which means to rub or daub in Middle Chinese. *Cha*, which means tea, is also from Middle Chinese. The combined word with these two parts is recorded as a Japanese-origin word. This word entered the OED relatively recently in 2016. *Matcha* refers to powdered green tea leaves which are added to hot water to make tea or used as a flavouring in desserts. These words are also used in their Anglicised, romanised forms in other European languages as shown in the following Twitter example (Figure 2.5).

2.9.7 Hot pot

Like *soy* and *tofu*, *hot pot* is used to refer to Pan-Asian cuisine. In the OED, *hot pot* was used to refer to British cuisine before it began to refer to East Asian foods. Now, it generally refers to a dish consisting of thinly sliced meat, vegetables, and other ingredients dipped in boiling stock by the diner at the table, or a metal pot used for cooking or

Figure 2.5 Matcha on Twitter.

serving such a dish. There is also the phrase *Mongolian hot pot* which refers specifically to a similar dish traditionally cooked in Mongolia:

> 1967 E. HUNT *Danger Game* viii. 152 He ate oysters at Lo Fan Shan and Mongolian Hotpot.

According to the corpus of GloWbE, *hot pot* has a per mille value of 1.43 in Hong Kong English, 0.49 in Singaporean English, and 0.1 in Australian English. *Hot pot* was popular in these three varieties of English. East Asian-origin food words are, in general, most popular in Southeast Asian varieties of English and Australian English with a few exceptions, such as *chopstick*.

2.9.8 Curry in the UK and Japan

The word *curry* first appeared in the OED in a culinary context in 1598. At the time of introduction, it took the definition of "a preparation of meat, fish, fruit, or vegetables, cooked with a quantity of bruised spices and turmeric, and used as a relish or flavouring, esp. for dishes composed of or served with rice". The noun *curry* was used to describe "a dish or stew flavoured with this preparation (or with curry powder)".

The term is listed by the OED as being of Tamil or Kannada origin, where *kari* and *karil* are terms for a sauce or relish for rice. The word probably entered British English via French and Portuguese usage. However, the use of the word *curry* in the English lexicon has come to mean almost any sauce-based Indian dish, and does not describe any particular flavour beyond the distinctive spices of the Indian subcontinent. *Curry* (or *kari*) in its indigenous usage has a meaning roughly equivalent to *gravy* in English, and hence it is rarely used to refer to a specific dish. For example, where an English menu may say 'chicken curry' or 'paneer (cheese) curry', a local description would be more inclined to distinguish between the specific dishes or flavours, referring to them as 'chicken masala' or 'matar paneer' instead.

The adaptation of the term *curry* into the English language, and the accompanying fondness for Indian cuisine (as homogenised under the aforementioned term), has spread to other languages, most clearly seen in the Japanese adaptation of curry (*karē*). Curry was introduced to Japan by the British during the Meiji era (1868–1912). India was under the colonial rule of the British at the time, and the use of boxed 'curry powder' as a flavouring or seasoning was popular among British troops; hence, it is spread to Japan through the military. 'Authentic' Japanese *karē* recipes differ greatly from their Indian originators due to their consistent use of curry sauce mix or boxed curry powder, and the frequent addition of sweet seasonings such as ketchup or apricot jam.

2.9.9 Bulgogi

Bulgogi is a Korean term referring to a dish of thinly sliced and marinated meet grilled on a barbecue or griddle, coming from the Korean terms for fire (*bul*) and meat (*gogi*). Despite becoming popular in the British food scene, *bulgogi* is yet to enter the OED. It does, however, appear in the Merriam-Webster dictionary with the definition of "a Korean dish of thinly sliced, marinated beef that is grilled or pan-fried", and is listed with a first known use of 1961. The first appearance of the term *bulgogi* in US and UK news was in 1978 and 1988, respectively; a lag which, along with the absence of the term in the OED, can be read as indicative of the greater influence of Korean immigrants and culture on the USA. It is also interesting to note that in both countries the initial appearance of *bulgogi* in the press was either italicised or in quotation marks, showing how Asian-origin words take a few years to transform from clear transliterations of another language, to a term actually considered part of the English lexicon, and therefore not requiring explanation or emphasis through orthographic representation.

The term in English has become increasingly popular online and in recipe books as Korean cuisine receives greater worldwide recognition. The dish (or variations thereof) now even features on restaurant menus and supermarket shelves across the UK. Interestingly, the term in English has come to refer not so much to the dish itself, but rather to indicate the marinade or sauce used in Korean-style grilled meats. For example, in Tesco supermarkets one can find a *Street Kitchen Korean Bulgogi Meal Kit*, consisting of a sachet carrying the description "enriched with soy and a distinctive blend of spices, this stir-fry sauce is simplicity at its best. To be enjoyed by everyone with their choice of meat and/or vegetables". This is an example of the transition of the original Korean term referring to grilled meats into an English term referring to a sauce with a certain flavour profile. This transition is also reflected in the recommendation that bulgogi sauce is to be enjoyed in stir fries or with a 'choice of meat and/or vegetables', indicating the adaptation of the traditional beef or pork dish to suit a greater variety of Western palates. Google Trends shows that while worldwide searches for beef bulgogi have increased at a far higher rate than other meats, searches for chicken bulgogi have come to outweigh those for the more traditional pork variety, revealing an adaptation of the dish to more international tastes.

Curry and *bulgogi* have made a similar transition from terms referring to general dishes, to those referring to sauces and flavourings within the English lexicon. The above description of the use of *bulgogi* sauce and marinade is almost directly comparable to the popularity of curry sauce in the UK. As the population became familiar with curry as a dish, as well as Indian restaurants (otherwise known as *curry houses*, also a term found in the OED dating back to 1883), curry sauce became a staple on British fish and chip shop menus across the nation. This adaptation of the term *curry* to mean a sauce with a certain flavour profile redolent of Indian cookery, rather than a curry dish itself, mirrors the transition of the term *bulgogi* into the English lexicon. Both terms have come to reference a homogenised set of seasonings and flavours, enabling them to be adapted into dishes more suited to international tastes.

2.9.10 Satay and satay sauce

Satay as a term in the OED dates back to 1934, defined as "an Indonesian and Malaysian dish, consisting of small pieces of meat grilled on a skewer and usually served with a spiced sauce". This mirrors the original meaning of the term to refer to meat cooked in a certain way. However, in the English lexicon the term *satay* is increasingly used to refer to a sauce often served with Southeast Asian grilled meats (or the seasonings and flavour profile therein). For example, in a grocery search of the Tesco website, five of the eleven results are described as 'satay sauce', two are satay sauce dressed noodles, and one is listed as 'satay seasoning'; in fact, only one result actually features meat on skewers. Of the five varieties of 'satay sauce', two of them are described as 'stir-fry sauce', not as sauce to put on grilled meat or skewers of any kind. Similarly, when searching Instagram for posts with the hashtag #satay, only half of the images featured skewered meats, while the other half featured dishes with satay sauce, dressing, or seasonings. Therefore, the development of the term *satay* in the English language is similar to that of *curry* and *bulgogi*: the term for a dish (or group of dishes) has been altered to refer to a certain kind of sauce or seasoning to enable its adaptation to international tastes.

2.9.11 Banh mi

Currently, there are 15 words from Vietnamese in the OED, including four food words. *Banh mi* refers to Vietnamese sandwiches. Vietnamese *bánh mì* became simplified as *bahn mi* in English. The OED defines *bahn mi* as below:

> In Vietnamese cuisine: a sandwich comprising a baguette (traditionally baked using a combination of rice and wheat flour) split lengthwise and filled with a variety of ingredients, typically including pâté and/or grilled meat, pickled vegetables, sliced chilli or chilli sauce, and fresh coriander. Also occasionally: a baguette loaf of the type used in such a sandwich.

The Merriam-Webster also defines *banh mi* as "a usually spicy sandwich in Vietnamese cuisine consisting of a split baguette filled typically with meat (such as pork or chicken) and pickled vegetables (such as carrot and daikon) and garnished with cilantro and often cucumbers". An article from the *New York Times* (2009) describes *banh mi* as "the classic street-vendor Vietnamese-French sandwich", which demonstrates the French culinary influence in Vietnamese foods such as *banh mi* and *pho*.[7]

2.9.12 Chao tom

This word is derived from the Vietnamese *chạo tôm*. It is defined in the OED as follows:

> In Vietnamese cookery: an appetizer consisting of pieces of minced shrimp (cf. surimi n.) held on sticks of sugar cane, and grilled or fried.

The first quote is found in 1969:

> 1969 R. Briand No Tears to Flow viii. 75 We all sat… to eat the delicious Vietnamese food… There was Cha Gio, tiny rolls with seafood and vermicelli… Then came Chao Tom, shrimp rolled around sugar cane and broiled.

It is noticeable that many first-generation non-Chinese and Japanese food words from East Asia entered English relatively late, in the late twentieth century.

2.9.13 Nuoc mam

According to the OED, *nuoc mam* is also Vietnamese. It refers to a sauce made from fermented fish. In the past, *fish sauce* was used to refer to diverse fish-based sauces. Now, new names are transliterated and enter into the English lexicon. These can boost the sense of authenticity surrounding individual foods, and the dining experience overall. The first quote using the word *nuoc man* is found in 1847:

> 1847 Chinese Repository Dec. 597 They most often eat it [sc. rice] with a bad ragout of fish, pungent beans, and a water of very salt fish, which they call nuoc mam.

According to GloWbE, *nuoc mam* is found most frequently in Singaporean and Australian Englishes.

2.9.14 Pho

In the OED, it is noted that the word *pho* is from the Vietnamese *phở*. It is defined as a type of Vietnamese soup, usually made from a beef bone stock and spices with noodles and thinly sliced beef or chicken added.

52 *First-generation food words*

Figure 2.6 Pho in different languages on Twitter.

The word *pho* is used mostly in Southeast Asian varieties of English, but it is also frequently found in Australian and US Englishes:

> 1935 'M. Morphy' Recipes All Nations 802 Pho is the name of an Annamese soup held in high regard. It is made with beef, a veal bone, onions, a bayleaf, salt, and pepper, and a small teaspoon of nuoc-man.

Pho is also found in French and German as shown below (Figure 2.6).

2.10 Summary

This chapter has illustrated the diversity and common ground among first-generation translingual food words from East Asia. The food words discussed herein have moved between multiple languages via many different routes, with their forms and meanings changing as they travel. Sometimes, they return to their language of origin as 'boomerang' words; sometimes they enter other European languages via English, while retaining an Anglicised spelling. The strategies for introducing these words into English have varied, including calquing, various forms of romanisation, and translation. We have also seen how the introduction of East Asian culinary vocabulary has affected English, with words such as dumpling taking on new meanings. There is even regional variation among the different Englishes of the UK, the USA, and Australia regarding the type of vocabulary received, and the meanings assigned to East Asian-origin words. This first generation of translingual food words is now firmly settled in English, but there is still uncertainty among the general public about some of these words' meanings.

Notes

1 https://assets.publishing.service.gov.uk/government/uploads/system/uploads/attachment_data/file/816781/ROMANIZATION_OF_MONGOLIAN.pdf (accessed 18 November 2019).
2 In spite of its Hokkien name, this dish is most common in Malaysian and Singaporean cookery.
3 The exact etymology of this word is unclear, as it may be traced to Malay, as well as Chinese.
4 This is also commonly seen without the accented 'é'.
5 This is also commonly seen without the '-'.
6 Other languages may have their unique strategy for new words. Here, I showcase German.
7 www.nytimes.com/2009/04/08/dining/08banh.html.

3 Fusion, localisation, and hybridity
Second-generation food words

Hybrid words are essential in our multicultural society to cater to word users' diverse needs to express and share their linguistic and cultural experiences. This chapter deals with the birth and rise of fusion cuisine and hybrid culinary words from the mid-twentieth century until now. In this chapter, I discuss how locally made hybrid and second-generation food words containing English fragments can enter English. Drawing on evidence from dictionaries, the corpus of Global Web-Based English (GloWbE), and social media, I trace the dynamic lives of second-generation food words of East Asian origin in English.

Second-generation words are locally produced terms with foreign elements (Kiaer and Bordilovskaya, 2017). This reflects human demographics: after first-generation immigrants have settled, the second-generation members are born and grow in the new home country. The second-generation members include in their vocabulary hybrid words made through the compounding, derivation, and blending of English and East Asian words. Hybrid terms are particularly abundant in the culinary sphere, perhaps because of the high frequency of intercultural interaction related to food.

When entering other languages, many English words are either translated or transliterated. Particularly in recent years, English words enter Asian languages in their romanised forms (Chapter 5). Second-generation food words are therefore much more visible in local East Asian languages. Increased contact with, and growing awareness of, East Asian culture has led to a rise in second-generation words entering English, and their further reshaping as global words. For instance, K-pop and J-pop have popularised many locally made second-generation words in their worldwide fandoms.

The growth of second-generation English words in East Asia implies an increased influence of English in the region. Typically, many second-generation words are born in so-called Outer Circle Englishes, such as Southeast Asian Englishes. However, as English is recognised as a source of social mobility in East Asia, and the general public's awareness of the English language has grown, more and more second-generation words are being produced in regions like China, Japan, and Korea, where English is not an official language. Second-generation words are often criticised as illegitimate or non-standard varieties by both local language authorities and English language authorities. However, Kiaer and Bordilovskaya (2017) argue that second-generation and hybrid English words are an asset for global English.

Second-generation hybrid words are growing quickly in regions with increased global language contacts, particularly through English. Korea and Japan are well known for their hybrid English words. Another hot location for hybrid words is Hong Kong, and Hong Kong-made words are particularly popular in Southeast Asian varieties of English.

3.1 The birth of hybrid and second-generation food words: methods of word-making

Second-generation hybrid words are made through compounding, derivation, or blending. Compounding simply means to put two words together. For instance, 'sunglasses' is a word in which 'sun' and 'glasses' are combined. Derivation involves adding a prefix or a suffix to an existing word to create a new, related term. For example, 'outpatient' is a combination of 'out' and 'patient', in which 'out' plays the role of prefix. Blending is the process of combining parts of two words to make one word, as in the case of 'smog'. The word 'smog' is made up of 'sm-' from 'smoke' and '-og' from 'fog'. Most Japanese- or Korean-English hybrid words are made through derivation and blending. However, Hong Kong-born hybrid words are often made through compounding. Calqued words such as *steamboat, dragon boat, Peking duck*, and *moon cake* can be viewed as first-generation words, but could also be understood as second-generation words due to the hybrid context in which they came to exist.

Despite the fact that second-generation words form an important part of the daily lexicon in Korean, treatment of these words has been negative both locally and internationally. The National Institute of Korean Language (NIKL) publishes a monthly list of words that need purification, most of which are second-generation hybrid English-Korean words (Kiaer, 2014a). This is because second-generation words are seen as a threat to the Korean language, and the NIKL dictionaries are therefore reluctant to include them as entries. Only 6% of the words in the NIKL dictionaries are foreign-origin – mainly English-origin – words (Kiaer, 2014a: 49). However, other dictionaries and media have a more open and inclusive attitude towards second-generation English words.

Treatment of these words by English speakers is not much better. Second-generation hybrid words are largely regarded as incorrect and illegitimate forms of English (Ahn, 2014; Kiaer, 2019a). However, Kiaer and Bordilovskaya (2017) propose that these hybrid English words accurately and effectively present unique Korean-ness, and argue that it is unreasonable to correct their use to conform to Inner Circle English norms.

Official Inner Circle English grammars cannot dictate the correct uses of second-generation words in English, as in the case of *phojito*, mentioned below. Similarly, Koreans rarely include inflectional affixes when they adopt English words into their lexicon. Therefore, *iced tea* becomes *ice tea*,[1] and *high heels* becomes *high heel*. Likewise, *frying pan* becomes *fry pan* and *curried rice* becomes *curry rice*.

3.2 Linguistic landscape shift: from Chinese to English

The entry of English in the late nineteenth century radically changed the linguistic landscapes of East Asia. Notably, written English started to play the role which Chinese characters had played for a long period of time. English became the language of prestige. Many writers and academics in this period came to admire English, and often expressed a view that the use of Classical Chinese characters had been a cause of the region's slow modernisation. This line of thinking was often expressed in political debates on national language. While it may be exaggerating to say that English has replaced Chinese in East Asia linguistically, English has been hugely influential in the region for approximately the last 120 years, especially in Japan and Korea. Nowadays in Korea, young children know fewer Sino-origin words, and grow up with more English words. The importance of learning English from a young age is never underestimated, but the practice of teaching children Chinese characters is constantly challenged. Chinese characters are gradually disappearing from official documents, signboards, brand names, textbooks, newspapers, and beyond. Meanwhile, the English alphabet is appearing more frequently (Kiaer, 2014a).

3.3 Hong Kong English

In Hong Kong English, some words describe aspects of life and culture unique to Hong Kong and have limited currency in other varieties of English, but others are used in various countries in the region with large Chinese communities, such as Singapore or Malaysia. English words have been coined in Hong Kong using various methods. There are analogical constructions such as *mini-hall* and *mini-flat*, and clippings such as *aircon* (an abbreviation of air conditioner). Acronyms are also very common, with ABC used to refer to American-born Chinese, and MTR to Mass Transit Rail.

Hong Kong English shows borrowing from Chinese and other languages, and loan translations including *almond cream, banana, bitter melon, chicken,* and *crystal bun*. Additionally, some words that exist in American or British English have come to have a modified meaning in Hong Kong English, such as *aunty, bath,* or *cheeky* (in Hong Kong English this means 'behaviour intended to cause, or resulting in, the provocation of violence'). A small percentage of words preserve archaic usages of English, such as *conservancy*, used as an alternative to conservation. Some words are used in modified grammatical forms, particularly treating mass nouns in British English as count nouns in Hong Kong English (Cummings and Wolf, 2011). This is particularly interesting to note given that when words from East Asian languages without obligatory number marking enter English, they are anglicised and number marking becomes obligatory. Singular-plural distinctions therefore exemplify the kind of grammatical terrain with which second-generation and hybrid words must grapple.

3.3.1 Historical background of Pan-Asian words in Hong Kong English

A number of words in Hong Kong English are of Anglo-Indian origin (such as *bungalow, chit, chop, congee,* and *mango*), a result of historical connections between India and Indian communities in Singapore, Malaya, and colonial Hong Kong. However, the number of Anglo-Indian words used today is relatively small.

A substantial number of Hong Kong words are also used in Singapore. There are several reasons for this. Historically, Hong Kong was a transit point for many Chinese emigrants from Guandong and Fujian provinces who were recruited as unskilled workers in the 'coolie' trade system in the nineteenth and early twentieth centuries. Chinese merchants and traders in Singapore and the Straits Settlements (Malacca,

Dindings, and Penang) had strong contacts with Hong Kong traders. More recently, Hong Kong families often have relatives living in Singapore, and there are many business transactions between the two cities, and with Malaysia. There are many Malaysian Chinese who visit Hong Kong every year, as well as Hongkongers who go to Singapore or Kuala Lumpur. English is used alongside, or instead of, Chinese to communicate with each other.

3.4 Case studies

In this section, I introduce the translingual journeys of different second-generation food words born from English and East Asian interactions. Interestingly, although many second-generation and hybrid food words of East Asian origin have enough textual evidence to qualify, they are not included in the OED. For example, we cannot find words such as *pork chop bun*, *pineapple cake*, or *egg tart*, despite their popularity and qualifications (they can even be found in academic texts, such as those on JSTOR). The East Asian-origin food words in the OED are limited to first-generation words only.

The following case studies illustrate how locally made words present different forms, meanings, and identities from their parent words. As with first-generation translingual food words, their journeys between languages are diverse and complex. Second-generation and hybrid food words also demonstrate the innovative treatment of foreign-origin words as they are adapted to local uses, and the impact of globalisation as seen through the growing variety of fusion cuisine.

3.4.1 Chimaek and somaek

The recently coined Korean-origin word *chimaek* (치맥, 'chicken with beer') illustrates how Korean culinary terms can gain prominence globally. The Korean word *chikin* (치킨, 'chicken') is originally from English, but in South Korea it is used exclusively to refer to a particular type of fried chicken. Nowadays, Korean-style fried chicken is becoming popular worldwide, and *chimaek*, a blend of *chi-* from *chikin* and *maek-* from *maekju* (맥주, 'beer'), has started to appear on the global culinary scene. This aspect of Korean food culture now not only is popular in Korea but has also begun to catch on abroad, particularly in mainland China and Taiwan. Some argue that the *chimaek* wave in China was sparked by the line "a snowy day is just perfect for our *chimaek* time" from the popular South Korean TV drama *My Love from the Star*. Restaurants selling *chimaek* have also started to

Figure 3.1 Somaek on Twitter.

appear in the UK, and are rapidly gaining popularity. As the hybrid word *chimaek* gains popularity and recognition around the world, it is in the process of becoming a global word. The word *somaek* (소맥), a combination of *so-* from *soju* (소주, a rice-based spirit) and *maek-* from *maekju*, referring to a mixed drink combining the two, is also frequently found in Twitter and newspapers (Figure 3.1).

3.4.2 Pho Salad: from soup to salad?

Pho (or *phở*) is a Vietnamese word thought to originate from the French *feu*, meaning 'stew'. It is defined by the OED as "A type of Vietnamese soup, usually made from a beef bone stock and spices with noodles and thinly sliced beef or chicken added". The word first appeared in an English language publication in 1935, in a recipe of the time describing *pho* as an "Annamese soup held in high regard". Google Trends shows that the worldwide popularity of the term *pho* increased between roughly 2007 and 2012, and has held a steady level of search popularity since. Despite being a soup in its original form, *pho* has become a part of the English culinary lexicon and sphere of understanding to the extent that it has been adapted and used in hybrid

60 Second-generation food words

phrases and dishes more suited to Western tastes. New terms such as *pho salad* have started to appear. Searches for *pho salad*, however, are mainly limited to Western countries, with Google Trends listing the search regions of Australia, Canada, the USA, and the UK only. This shows that when words like *pho* enter the English lexicon and become increasingly popular, they are more liable to adaptation and hybridisation into new forms.

3.4.3 Phojito

This is a word found in Vietnamese restaurants in the West combing *pho-* and *-jito*, possibly from *mojito*. The pronunciation of this word is hard to judge, and cannot be dictated by 'single' English grammar (Figure 3.2).

It is particularly interesting to note in this example the way in which a second-generation English word is made by combining first-generation words from two distinct languages, both of which have been accepted to the extent that an English-speaking customer can be presumed to understand a hybrid term combining Vietnamese and Cuban culinary terms. This exemplifies the degree of hybridisation that can occur in a region which has experienced multiple forms of language contact.

Figure 3.2 Phojito on Twitter.

3.4.4 Matcha latte: is latte coffee or milk?

The term *matcha* entered the English lexicon over a 100 years ago, and in recent years it has become an increasingly trendy food in the Western culinary scene. *Matcha* is listed in the OED with the definition of "powdered green tea leaves which are added to hot water to make tea or used as a flavouring in desserts". While the English term comes directly from the Japanese word *matcha*, meaning a powdered green tea, the mention of it as a flavouring in desserts in the dictionary definition shows the importance of modern food trends to the word's popularity, and reveals this as the main form through which *matcha* has entered the English lexicon.

Despite its relatively long history in the OED (with usage listing back to 1881), the term has only recently found a comfortable place in the lexicon as an English term in its own right. This is evidenced by the numerous different spellings of the term in English-language publications (*matcha, macha, maccha, mat-cha,* among others), as well as the habitual use of quotation marks and italicisation.

The word *latte* has a far more recent entry in the OED. While the phrase *caffè latte* first appeared in 1847, the *latte* was first listed with its own entry as late as 1989. *Caffè latte* originates from the Italian *caffè latte* (lit. milk coffee), and is described as a "Coffee made with milk, esp. hot or steamed milk". The term *latte* has exactly the same dictionary definition, revealing that nowadays *latte* indicates the type of coffee-based drink, rather than its original meaning of 'milk'.

The term *matcha latte* has seen an incredible rise in popularity in recent years. It refers to a drink similar to a *caffè latte*, but instead of the coffee (or *caffè*) element, the drink is made with matcha green tea and milk. Essentially, it is a drink made of (often hot or steamed) milk flavoured with matcha green tea powder. When used together, the terms *matcha* and *latte* form a hybrid term to describe an equally hybrid drink, combining a flavour originating in East Asia co-opted into a popular Italian drink. While the term *latte* instantly makes one think of coffee in an English context, *latte* when used with *matcha*, even in an English context, refers to a hot frothy milk drink rather than coffee.[2] This then leaves us with the question of which language we should consider the term *matcha latte* to belong to. One may at first glance consider it to be an English term due to its popularity and hybridisation in the West. However, the use of the term *latte*, stripped of its link to coffee and instead meaning just 'milk', could mean we should consider it as coming directly from its original Italian meaning, hence making the term *matcha latte*[3] a direct hybrid of Japanese and

Italian origins with added identity of English. Google Trends shows the worldwide popularity of the term increasing greatly between the late 2000s and the present, with the most popular search region by far being Singapore. This suggests that Southeast Asian Englishes also have a role to play in the consideration and classification of the term.

3.4.5 *Pineapple cake*

Pineapple cake is a Taiwanese sweet delicacy often written as 鳳梨酥 (*fēnglísū*) in traditional Chinese characters. It is also sometimes written as 王梨酥 and romanised under Pe̍h-ōe-jī as *ông-lâi-so*. Pineapple is a foreign fruit, speculated to have been introduced to Japan by Portuguese settlers before being introduced by the Japanese to Taiwan, so there is significant dialectical variation in Chinese words for pineapple. The term *ông-lâi* (王梨) is a dialectical word for pineapple mostly prevalent in Hokkien, which is spoken primarily in Taiwan and mainland China's Fujian province, as well as some smaller areas in Southern China. 风梨 *fènglí* is also used primarily in Taiwan to refer to pineapple. However, in most parts of mainland China, including Beijing, 菠萝 *bōluó* is used to mean 'pineapple'. Pineapple – and pineapple cake – has strong symbolic meaning within Taiwanese culture, likely a contributing factor to their popularity with Taiwanese people and tourists alike.

The history of the pineapple cake stretches back to the Three Kingdoms period in China. After the fall of the Han Dynasty, the kingdoms of Wei, Shu, and Wu remained. Shu and Wu wished to unite and overthrow the powerful kingdom of Wei, so the emperor of Shu married the younger sister of the emperor of Wu. Along with other engagement gifts, Shu's emperor sent a pineapple cake. The word for pineapple in Taiwanese Hokkien, *ông-lâi*, sounds phonologically similar to a phrase that means 'prosperity arrives' or 'go forth and prosper', which conveys the idea that many children will be born into a family. As a result of this, they are often given as engagement gifts. The cake later evolved beyond an engagement treat to become a representative Taiwanese delicacy.

Despite historically being a Taiwanese ceremonial treat, Google's search feature shows the overwhelming prominence of the English translation of *pineapple cake* over the romanised forms of *fēnglísū* or *ông-lâi-so*. One potential reason could be the immense popularity of pineapple cake among Japanese tourists. In Japanese, it is transcribed using *katakana* script as パイナップルケーキ *painappuru kēki*. Pineapple has been known to grow in Taiwan since as early as the seventeenth century, but it wasn't until Japanese occupation in the nineteenth century that Taiwan became the third largest producer of pineapples in the world. Japan's role in the introduction of pineapples to Taiwan may have contributed to the popularity of the term *pineapple cake* – which is close to パイナップルケーキ *painappuru kēki* – as opposed to Chinese forms.

3.4.6 Pork bun

The Pork Chop Bun (猪扒包 *zhūbā bāo* in Mandarin) is a popular street snack on the island of Macau. The dish features a thinly sliced and fried pork chop inside a bread roll often called a 'piggy bun' (豬仔包, *zhū zǎi bāo*), sometimes also with lettuce, tomatoes, pickles, or sauces. The origins of the bun's two components lie in the Portuguese occupation of Macau and consequent culinary influence. The frying of a piece of meat (with little to no particular seasonings) is redolent of Mediterranean cuisine, while the 'piggy bun' is a baguette-like bread roll commonly found in Brazil, Macau, and Hong Kong, all places influenced by Portuguese colonialism. The use of the term '包' (*bāo*) to describe a Western-style bun is a common practice all over the Chinese-speaking world, showing how the word (originally used to describe traditional Chinese steamed dough products, such as filled buns) has been adapted to describe altogether different Western-style baked goods.

It should be noted that culinary terms from Macau which show Portuguese origin are hardly found in English. Some very well-known food words such as *arroz bacalhau*, *arroz doce*, or *Pasteis de Nata* are romanised yet hardly used in English. Macau- and *Portuguese Egg tart* are the only terms which have successfully entered English.

3.4.7 Tǔsī

Tǔsī (土司) is a very common food word in Taiwan, seen every day and on almost every street. *Tǔsī* refers to a kind of sandwich made with slightly sweet, American-style sliced white bread, which can either be toasted or, as is more common, simply filled, sliced diagonally, and served for breakfast. Given its use in this dish, the term *tǔsī* has also come to refer to the specific kind of bread itself, sold in pre-sliced loaves in nearly every supermarket in Taiwanese cities. The word originates from the English word *toast*, but it is clear that the meaning is very different here. Rather than retaining the English meaning of 'toasted bread', the word *tǔsī* in Taiwan commonly refers to a whole sandwich or a kind of sliced bread (usually not toasted at all), showing the development of the term into a whole new word in Taiwanese

64 Second-generation food words

Mandarin. The sandwiches themselves have become a staple in Taiwanese street breakfast stalls, and this product is becoming incredibly hybridised, featuring fillings combining Chinese tastes with US influences, such as bacon with Chinese-style omelette. A similar breakfast item can be found in South Korea. For example, the chain restaurant Isaac Toast (이삭토스트 *Isak toseuteu*) serves breakfast sandwiches which are named on the menu as '토스트' (*toseuteu*) from the English 'toast'. For example, one can order the 'Bulgogi mvp' (불고기 mvp 토스트, *Bulgogi mvp toseuteu*), which highlights in both name and content the hybridity of this food item.

3.4.8 QQ

The notion of *Q* (often duplicated as *QQ*) in Chinese is difficult to describe in a Western culinary context. The term is used to refer to foods with a certain pleasant chewiness or glutinous mouthfeel, a far more prized texture in Asian foods than in Western cuisines. It is often used to describe items such as chewy or rubbery noodles, fish balls, and glutinous rice cakes. The term itself stems from a similar sounding Hokkien term meaning 'chewy', but it appropriates the Western letter *Q* (pronounced *qiū*) in its written form, appearing on restaurant signs and menus around Taiwan.[4] Assigning a Roman letter to a concept so unique to Asian cuisine and tastes (so much so that it is virtually absent in Western cuisines) provides an excellent example of the depth of language borrowing in Taiwan. The term *Q* is even seen in small Chinese-speaking restaurants, where it is the only Roman letter on a menu of exclusively Chinese-language dishes, showing the extent to which the word has penetrated the local lexicon. *QQ* has also begun to appear beyond an East Asian context; there is a popular bubble tea chain called 'Chatime' which has branches around the world, including Taiwan and the UK, and offers a series of *QQ* beverages. The term can now be seen on global social media platforms (Figure 3.3).

Figure 3.3 'QQ' on Twitter.

3.4.9 Egg tarts

The Mandarin and Cantonese term for egg tarts – 蛋挞 romanised as *daahn tāat* in Cantonese, and *dàntǎ* in Mandarin – is a perfect example of a hybrid term taking hold in an Asian lexicon. Believed to have been developed in Hong Kong in the 1940s as an adaptation of the Portuguese *pastel de nata*, which is popular in Macau, the term is a hybrid of the Chinese word for egg (蛋, *dàn*) and the English word *tart*. The term is especially appropriate as it refers to the Western origins of the 'tart', while also indicating the Chinese adaptation of the pastry featuring the addition of a greater quantity of egg into the custard mix, which distinguishes it from its European counterpart.

3.4.10 Yōshoku

As discussed in Chapter 2, the *yōshoku* (Western food) genre of food found in Japan refers to a style of Western-influenced cooking originating in the Meiji period. In Japan and Korea, *yōshoku* terms are seen as Western food names, while in the West they are considered Western-influenced Japanese food. *Yōshoku* primarily consists of Japanised forms of European dishes, with Western names that are often written in *katakana*. For example, *omuraisu* is a blend of *omelette* and *rice*. Other popular *yōshoku* dishes include *hamburg steak*, *ton katsu* (pork cutlet), and *beef katsu* (beef cutlet) among others.

3.4.11 Royal milk tea from milk tea

The term *milk tea* was originally assembled in Hong Kong to describe a type of tea made with milk or cream. It was formed as a calqued translation from the Cantonese 奶茶 (*náaih*, 'milk' and *chàh*, 'tea'), and is used mainly in Southeast Asian varieties of English (Figure 3.4).

In the OED, *milk tea* is defined as

> any of various drinks made with tea and milk or cream; esp. a drink originating in Hong Kong, made with black tea and evaporated or condensed milk. [In use with reference to China after Chinese (Mandarin) nǎichá (1885 or earlier; < nǎi milk + chá tea: see CHA n.), in use with specific reference to Hong Kong after its Cantonese equivalent náaih chàh.

CHANGE TO VERTICAL CHART / CLICK TO SEE CONTEXT

SECTION	ALL	US	CA	GB	IE	AU	NZ	IN	LK	PK	BD	SG	MY	PH	HK	ZA	NG	GH	KE	TZ	JM
FREQ	356	36	16	10	1	19	3	6	10	2	7	55	27	81	73	0	0	0	4	6	0
WORDS (M)	1900	386.8	134.8	387.6	101.0	148.2	81.4	96.4	46.6	51.4	39.5	43.0	41.6	43.2	40.5	45.4	42.6	38.8	41.1	35.2	39.6
PER MIL	0.19	0.09	0.12	0.03	0.01	0.13	0.04	0.06	0.21	0.04	0.18	1.28	0.65	1.87	1.80	0.00	0.00	0.00	0.10	0.17	0.00

Figure 3.4 'Milk tea' in Global Web-Based English (GloWbE).

The first quotation is found as below:

> 1897 *Cornhill Mag.* Mar. 176 A decoction known as *nai-ch'a*, or 'milk-tea', is drunk at the Manchu court, and is served out on state occasions.

After becoming popular, the drink made its way into Japan, where it was developed further. In Japan, the term *Royal Milk Tea* was used perhaps to add a connotation of specialness. The name of the drink is in English, but it was developed in Japan after originally being assembled in Hong Kong, and has since been developed further in Taiwan. Thus, it is difficult to label this drink as belonging to a single etymological origin.

3.4.12 Bibimbap salad

This term is a combination of the Korean *bibimbap* and the English 'salad'. Bibimbap refers to a dish of rice and a variety of mixed ingredients. In a Western setting, bibimbap salad recipes may use various Korean-influenced ingredients and seasonings such as sesame oil, *gochujang*, bean sprouts, and thinly sliced or ground meat. Although the 'bap' of bibimbap literally means rice, this fusion dish often replaces the rice with barley or quinoa, as seen in the Tweet below (Figure 3.5).

Figure 3.5 Bibimbap salad on Twitter.

68 *Second-generation food words*

3.4.13 Chinese tapas

This term is used to describe small dishes from Chinese cuisine, such as a platter of assorted starters, in an English-speaking context. The Spanish-origin word 'tapas' efficiently communicates the concept of small dishes to be shared, while at the same time adding an elegant and foreign nuance to the dish (Figure 3.6).

3.4.14 Shrimp twigim

Twigim is a deep-frying cooking method. Nowadays, people transliterate *twigim* despite the existence of other words that are close in meaning – notably *tempura*. This example illustrates that the choice of words is not just about expressing the meaning of individual terms. *Twigim* is used instead of *tempura* as a means of enabling word users to assert their identity and build empathy with those who are interested in Korean cuisine (Figure 3.7).

Figure 3.6 'Chinese Tapas' on Twitter.

Second-generation food words 69

> You may wonder if these Shrimp Twigim is similar to the Japanese style tempura. They are somewhat similar but...
>
> 4:00 pm · 4 Jan 2014

Figure 3.7 Shrimp *Twigim* on Twitter.

Figure 3.8 'Sushi burrito' on Twitter.

3.4.15 Sushi burrito

In this example, the Japanese *sushi* and Mexican *burrito* are combined in an English-speaking context. Western English speakers are likely to be more familiar with the term 'burrito' than the Japanese *ehomaki*, which is used to describe long sushi rolls. 'Burrito' also implies a fusion cuisine, and some varieties of sushi burrito include Mexican ingredients alongside the traditional Japanese flavours (Figure 3.8).

3.4.16 Yuzu ponzu sauce

Many sauce names are also second-generation words. *Yuzu ponzu sauce* includes the Japanese *yuzu* (a type of citrus fruit often used to flavour East Asian dishes) and *ponzu* (a sauce made with a combination of citrus fruit and soy sauce). Here we see a double repetition – the word *yuzu* describes the citrus flavouring already implied in the word *ponzu*, while the word 'sauce' translates *ponzu* for an audience who is not familiar with Japanese.

3.5 Summary

Second-generation and hybrid translingual food words exist in many forms. I have presented examples created in East Asian contexts from English components, many of which travel into English to become global words. Second-generation words are also created in English-language settings, using East Asian terms to describe fusion cuisine, and emphasise the 'exotic' nature of a particular dish. Examining the roots and translingual journeys of second-generation food terms reveals the historical interactions and contemporary links within and between East Asian and Western English-speaking countries. Although these terms are often considered less legitimate than first-generation food words by linguistic authorities, we can see from the examples above that second-generation food words enrich our vocabularies, playing an important expressive and descriptive role in our international, interconnected societies.

Notes

1. Countries such as the Netherlands also say *ice tea*, even though Dutch is inflected rather than agglutinative, and very closely related to English overall. Other continental European countries such as France use *ice tea* too.
2. It would be perfectly ok to use 'latte, please' in a coffee shop to mean café latte. In fact, it would be more natural to say *latte* only than *café latter* in ordering drinks.
3. In South Korea, there are many types of *latte* such as *Kokuma latte* (sweet potato latte) *Hong cha latte* (red tea latte).
4. https://taiwanlanguage.wordpress.com/2011/12/08/q (kiuʰ)—軟靭/ (accessed 18 November 2019).

4 Globalisation and social media
The global food words

In this chapter, I discuss how food terms start as local words before turning into global words. In particular, I explore the roles of globalisation and social media in birthing a new, global generation of food words. I discuss the processes through which words enter the global lexicon. Such processes include the straightforward borrowing of regional culinary words – first-generation words – as foods become known internationally for the first time. However, there also exist innovative terms that are born through hybridisation and fusion of food cultures and languages, as well as modified variants of long-standing terms, in this sense, second-generation words. Throughout the chapter, I seek to argue that globalisation, social media, and English as Lingua Franca (ELF) have challenged the lives of East Asia-born culinary words in English languages. As globalisation advances, the forms, meanings, and identities of these words are being reshaped, as they become part of a global lexicon.

4.1 Contextual factors in the making of global food words

4.1.1 Growth of the Asian population in the English-speaking world

The explosion in new food words in the English language is partly driven by the increasing linguistic and cultural diversity of major countries where English is the dominant language. As English comes into intense contact with speakers of many different languages, this creates an opportunity for the mutual exchange of food terms. In this section, I focus on the increase in the number of individuals with Asian heritage living in the English-speaking world in recent years.

72 Global food words

Increased global exchange, driven by commerce, migration, and online communication, means that our lives are ever more closely interwoven across national boundaries. As a direct result, new words are constantly being born out of this contact. No matter whether one has welcomed or resisted the situation, in all parts of the globe, the movement towards multilingual, multicultural societies is advancing at an unprecedented scope and speed (Vervotec, 2007).

In the English-speaking world, the Asian diaspora is growing particularly fast. In the case of the UK, the 2011 Census showed that the Asian or Asian British ethnic group category had one of the largest increases since 2001. Among the foreign-born population of England and Wales, 2.4 million, or a third of the total foreign-born population, identified as Asian British in 2011 (Office for National Statistics, 2013). This figure excludes Asian British people living in other constituent countries of the UK; the nationwide number, therefore, is even larger. Similarly, the 2011 US census bureau[1] found that Asian and Pacific Island languages form a major part of the languages spoken in the USA. These languages include: Chinese; Korean; Japanese; Vietnamese; Hmong; Khmer; Lao; Thai; Tagalog or Filipino; the Dravidian languages of India, such as Telugu, Tamil, and Malayalam; and other languages of Asia and the Pacific, including the Polynesian languages, Micronesian languages, and regional languages of the Philippines. Among these, Chinese, Korean, and Vietnamese belong to the top ten most widely spoken languages in the country, with the numbers of speakers continuing to rise rapidly.

The situation is similar in other English-speaking countries like Australia and Canada. In Australia, the top five foreign languages are Mandarin, Arabic, Cantonese, Vietnamese, and Italian. The top ten foreign languages also include Filipino/Tagalog, Hindi, and Punjabi. In Canada, Tagalog and Punjabi are growing rapidly.[2]

The increasing number of immigrants from Asia is exerting a greater linguistic and cultural influence in English-speaking countries. Culinary culture is one of the key factors that bind diaspora together; therefore, it is inevitable that the number of Asian-origin food words is also increasing in the English spoken in these countries.

4.1.2 Growth in Asian language learners in English-speaking countries

Alongside the increase in speakers of Asian languages residing in English-speaking countries, the number of English speakers learning selected Asian languages as a second language has also been on the rise.

These two trends are likely linked to an extent. First, the increasing number of individuals of second-generation Asian background in English-speaking countries may be motivated to study an Asian heritage language, even if their first language is English. Second, English speakers who have Asian-background friends or colleagues may become interested in an Asian culture and feel motivated to take up a language as a result. Regardless of the original motivation, as English speakers learn a whole host of Asian food-related vocabulary items in their language studies, this increases the likelihood that some of these words will enter the English lexicon.

Among Asian languages, a recent surge in the popularity of learning Korean has made news headlines across the English-speaking world. For example, the BBC reported in July 2018 that 14,000 students were learning Korean in the USA, up from 163 only two decades ago. Additionally, the Modern Language Association reported that the popularity of Korean courses in US universities increased by nearly 14% between 2013 and 2016, even though overall language enrolment declined during that period. The surge in enthusiasm for Korean learning is driven by the increased popularity of Korean popular culture like music and TV dramas in recent years, a trend commonly referred to as the 'Korean Wave' or *hallyu*.[3] While the Korean Wave originally spread regionally to neighbouring countries in East Asia and Southeast Asia, it has now gone global. As a result, it is increasingly common for individuals in the Anglosphere to be exposed to Korean popular culture. A prominent example is the Psy song *Gangnam Style*, which became a worldwide viral hit in 2012 and topped the music charts in English-speaking countries like the UK and Australia.

The rise in popularity in studying Asian languages is not limited to Korean. In 2018, the *Telegraph* reported that entries for Chinese A-level in the UK had overtaken German for the first time in history. This made Chinese the third most popular foreign language for UK students, with 3,334 examinees in that year, ranking behind only French and Spanish.[4] This illustrates how British children are increasingly given the opportunity to study an Asian language in secondary school, and are opting to pursue this study to a high level.

Outside of schools, self-study platforms also indicate strong demand for East Asian languages. As of October 2019, out of a total of 34 online language courses offered by *Duolingo* for English speakers, Japanese ranked fourth overall in popularity with over six million learners, surpassing major European languages like Italian, Russian, and Portuguese. Similarly, Korean put in a strong showing in sixth place (3.64 million learners) and Chinese came seventh (3.49 million learners).[5] These numbers indicate a strong base of English-speaking learners self-studying these languages.

As English-speaking learners pursue the study of Asian languages through universities, secondary schools, and self-teaching platforms, they are also more likely to encounter the cultures that speak these languages natively. Learners' encounters with Asian cultures will likely also touch upon food cultures. As a result, the surge in learners studying Asian languages can also be seen as a significant driving factor in the transmission of Asian food words into English.

4.1.3 Growth of the English-speaking population in East Asia

As the Asian-origin population has grown in the English-speaking world, the number of English speakers in East Asia has also grown rapidly over the last 20 years. In 2017, there were 55,713 residents of American nationality alone living in Japan.[6] Meanwhile, in Taiwan, there were a total of 9,605 residents from the USA, 2,070 from Canada, 2,008 from the UK, and 818 from Australia in August 2019.[7] One of the main causes for the growth in the English-speaking population is the demand for English teachers. To take an example, South Korean public schools employed 4,962 native English speakers from abroad as language teachers in 2016.[8]

4.1.4 Growth in English language learners in East Asia

The increase in the number of English teachers in East Asia reflects an increasing demand for English as a Foreign Language (EFL) tuition in the region. Indeed, the number of EFL speakers has also exploded in recent years. When Asian EFL learners come into contact with English, they generally bring elements of their native language to their English speech. This situation of language contact can be an important driver for the creation of new lexical items, including food words.

In the twenty-first century, where English serves as the global lingua franca, proficiency in English is an increasingly vital element of career success in business and academia. As a result, East Asian countries have been investing a great deal of time and financial resources into training young generations in using English. By producing populations that are bilingual in English and the national language, governments are aiming to prepare the next generation to compete in a globalised economic environment.

In countries including South Korea, parents spend vast sums of money on private tuition to try and ensure their child's proficiency in English. These private programmes are targeting children at an increasingly young age, bidding for the funds of parents who are seeking to provide their children with the earliest possible exposure to English. Indeed, the Ministry of Education and Statistics Korea found that in 2018, parents spent a total of 5.7 trillion won on private English education for their children, which was more than any other school subject.[9] The widespread zeal for EFL education at younger and younger ages, frequently referred to as 'English Fever', has reached such a level of intensity in South Korea that it is now viewed as a social problem. To take one example, the Moon Jae-in administration of the South Korean government has recently reviewed the idea of banning English education for preschool children.[10]

As younger Asian generations, taught in English throughout their school career, start to enter the world of work, the working populations of Asian countries are becoming increasingly proficient in the language. In 2012, ABC News reported that Asia had approximately 800 million English speakers, which is more than the population of the entire Anglosphere of native English-speaking countries put together. Of these 800 million English speakers, China alone had approximately 330 million.[11] These EFL learners often introduce features of their native languages into their English, producing what has been referred to as 'new Englishes' born through language contact. For example, common features of Chinese speakers' English include grammatical features like absence of the definite article, alongside phonological aspects like the merging of /l/ and /r/.[12] These speakers of new Asian Englishes, with their large population, have also served as significant creators of new English words including food terms in recent years.

4.1.5 English as an Asian lingua franca

In the case of Asia, an important part of the puzzle is not only English as a Foreign Language (EFL) but equally English as a Lingua Franca (ELF). In the twenty-first century, English is commonly used for communication between individuals in non-native English-speaking countries, where speakers who do not understand each other's mother tongues nonetheless have learned English as a second language. Such a situation of ELF is the norm not only in Europe but also in Asia, where there is no realistic competitor for cross-border lingua franca.

Across the East Asian cultural sphere, classical Chinese served as a written lingua franca in pre-modern times, having been employed by writers across China, Korea, Japan, and Vietnam. Throughout East Asian history, however, Chinese has never served as a spoken lingua franca for the region (Lurie, 2011). In contemporary times, even though Mandarin Chinese has 1.1 billion native speakers, they overwhelmingly live in just one country – the PRC.[13] Thus, Chinese is not well suited for the position of Asian lingua franca at the present moment.

During the era of the colonial Japan, Japanese was similarly used across national borders as the language of the colonial power. For example, Japanese was used as an official language for several decades during the Japanese rule over Taiwan (1895–1945) and Korea (1910–1945). However, the baggage of the colonial past has led to the discouragement of Japanese-learning in countries like South Korea in the post-war era. Instead, the USA established a military presence in many East Asian states after its victory in the Second World War, including in Japan itself. Partially as a result of these political factors, the most widely learned foreign language of the present era in East Asia is undoubtedly English.

While English is used as a lingua franca in Asia, the English spoken can be quite divergent from UK or US standard varieties of the language. As speakers introduce elements from their local languages and cultures into their English speech, there are often many locally born words or hybrid words with English components created.

The reality of English as a Lingua Franca (ELF) also reflects the multilingualism of the Asian population. Multilingualism itself is not a new phenomenon, with humans having lived with linguistic diversity for centuries. However, it does appear that multilingualism is holding up remarkably well in the modern day, with great swathes of the East Asian population having competency in multiple languages. Although there are no exact figures, it has been estimated that half of the world's population is bilingual (Grosjean, 2012).

Such a context, where individuals apply knowledge of multiple languages and cultures in their day-to-day lives, creates fertile ground for the development of new food words.

4.1.6 Growth in the tourism sector

The transnational use of English has also been bolstered by an explosion in worldwide tourist numbers over the previous few decades. Since the Second World War, the number of international tourists has grown exponentially.[14] According to research by the World Tourism Organization (UNTWO), there were 1.4 billion international tourist arrivals in 2018 – an all-time high.[15] In contrast, the number was only 166 million in 1970, and a mere 25 million in 1950. A sizeable number of these visits were made to predominantly English-speaking countries, with the US ranking as the third most visited country worldwide (77 million arrivals) and the UK coming in seventh (39 million arrivals).[16] As tourists from Asia explore the English-speaking world and its cuisine, they are increasingly coming into contact with the English language and being required to use the language in contexts relating to food. The occurrence of language contact on an unprecedented scale driven by rising tourist numbers creates conditions favourable for the creation of new food words.

Even when travel destinations fall outside of the Anglosphere, this can still fuel the transnational use of English on account of the ELF phenomenon. In the past, it was much more unusual for the general population to come into a situation where a transnational lingua franca was actually required. However, as more and more people experience international travel, finding a means of communication in restaurants and bars is becoming essential to these tourists. According to the UNTWO, Chinese people made more journeys abroad in 2017 than citizens of any other country (143 million journeys), and China was also the fourth most visited country in the world (61 million arrivals). Similarly, citizens of Japan and South Korea also travelled abroad for tourism in sizeable numbers.[17] As discussed previously, the most popular foreign language and the main international lingua franca in East Asia is English. As East Asian people travel to other countries in the region or beyond, it is increasingly advantageous for them to employ English for communication. This sets up the circumstances for greater international usage of English, and for linguistic innovation in the language.

4.1.7 English as a language of social media

In discussing the role of English as a lingua franca, it is also pertinent to discuss the effects of the World Wide Web and social media. The need to communicate with foreigners who had no knowledge of your country's language was often, in the recent past, limited to scenarios like overseas travel, which was expensive and strictly time-limited for most people. In contrast, the World Wide Web now provides opportunities to interact with people from all around the world on a regular basis, especially with the rise of internet forums and social networking sites. Accordingly, written English is omnipresent on the Internet as a way for people of various linguistic means to communicate with each other. In East Asia, Internet and mobile technologies are generally highly advanced. The economies of Japan and South Korea have been well known worldwide for their high-tech expertise for many decades, with China having recently also built up an impressive, globally competitive IT sector. In all of these countries, smartphones have been widely adopted. In this way, ordinary citizens in East Asia have the ability to access, create, and share words through their networked handheld devices.

In contrast to print media, there is very little administrative oversight of the language that is used online; it is impractical for the enormous amounts of text data uploaded to social media every single day to undergo centralised editorial oversight. Thus, Internet users are largely free to innovate, subvert prescribed norms, and incorporate elements of their native languages in their use of English online. As a result, social media becomes a hub for the creation of new words in the English language, including terms relating to food. In the following section, we provide examples of the use of food terms on social media, focusing on the creation and spread of these words.

4.2 Social media and global food word creation

As part of the methodology of this study, I have drawn up data collected primarily from social media through searching different lexical items. As there is comparatively little data that predate 2008, we will deal primarily with data from 2008 to present, namely, data from after the establishment of high-profile social media platforms like Facebook, Twitter, and Instagram.

One of the key aims of this book is to show how social media has played a role in the birth and growth of East Asian food words that are rapidly turning into translingual words. As briefly mentioned in Chapter 1, social media used by netizens across national and linguistic boundaries is ushering in a new era with a global lexicon. Throughout this section of the chapter, I seek to explain the processes on social media which are fuelling the creation and spread of food words.

Based on my analysis of social media posts, I identified seven major themes: translanguaging, non-verbal communication, influence of pop culture, social media language use as cultural capital, amplification of minority cultures, simplification of forms, and variants of words. I will now outline each of these themes in turn.

4.2.1 Translanguaging

In the social media content I examined, there were countless examples of the use of multiple languages within a single post, a phenomenon that has been named 'translanguaging'. The term 'translanguaging'

Global food words 79

originated in the 1980s, arising through research on the use of Welsh and English in bilingual classrooms in Wales (Lewis, Jones, and Baker, 2012), before becoming a research field in its own right (García and Wei, 2014). According to Williams (2002), 'translanguaging' refers to the receiving of information in one language and its subsequent application in another language. In this way, we see knowledge of food cultures acquired in one language applied in social media posts made in another language.

Cross-linguistically, it is common to see food words passing from one language to another with English serving as an intermediary. The examples below show tweets referencing *Peking duck* in Turkish and Russian, demonstrating how it is often the English food name that enters the global lexicon, even for food items that originate from non-English cultures (Figure 4.1).

As we saw in Chapter 2, most of the early East Asian food words entering other languages did so through English. In this way, English serves as a medium for the global spread of even non-English–origin words.

As globalisation accelerates, it will become increasingly common for culinary terms to start to lose their local association with only one specific language or culture. Already, some staple herbs like coriander, which was originally mainly used in Southeast Asian cuisine, are starting to be widely used in a global context and are losing their regional connotations. Likewise, methods like *stir-frying* or utensils like the *wok*, which were originally used in Asian cooking, can be widely used in European cuisine and beyond. In the past, *fish sauce* or *chilli sauce* could be enough information to specify a particular condiment. However, there are now many varieties of *fish sauce* or *chilli sauce* available in a globalised environment, meaning that the regional association is not strong enough to identify the specific sauce. As a result, it is becoming increasingly important to be more explicit about the

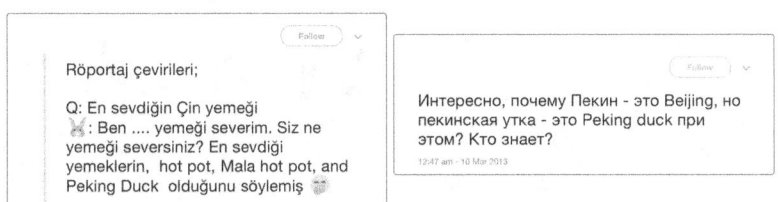

Figure 4.1 'Peking duck' in Turkish- and Russian-language tweets.

80 *Global food words*

sauce type. In this way, as food terms lose their association with a specific language or culture, it will be increasingly possible to see social media posts demonstrating translanguaging, simply drawing upon a pool of global words.

4.2.2 Non-verbal communication: images and emojis

Another prevalent feature of food-related social media posts is their use of non-verbal communication methods. For example, food-related emojis are commonly shared to add additional meanings to social media comments. These food emojis usually differ not by language, but by the device used to view the social media content. Below are some examples of food-related emojis on both iPhone and Samsung Galaxy mobile devices (Figures 4.2 and 4.3).

As can be seen, many emojis depict foods of Asian origin. It appears that users generally choose to use emojis to add expressive meanings like fun and playfulness. However, as the emojis are consistent across languages, they also serve as a useful, quick, and intuitive method of communicating, demolishing linguistic barriers. In the following example, we see emojis substituting words, with a chilli pepper in place of the adjective 'spicy' and a bowl of rice to represent the noun 'rice' (Figure 4.4).

Figure 4.2 Food-related emojis on iPhone.

Global food words 81

Figure 4.3 Food-related emojis on Samsung Galaxy.[18]

Figure 4.4 Emoji substituting for words.

82 *Global food words*

Figure 4.5 Food image sharing on Twitter.

Additionally, social media users complemented their posts using not only emojis but also image, audio and video file attachments. In this way, they can provide additional visual information for understanding the context of the post that is easily comprehensible regardless of language. Attaching images also seemed to add an expressive element of fun, allowing social media users to share their emotional experience with preparing or eating foods from around the world. Below is an example of a tweet with attached images adding expressive meaning (Figure 4.5).

4.2.3 Influence of pop culture on word popularity

Examination of food-related social media posts also revealed that the popularity of different words can be driven by pop culture trends and fandoms. There are multiple factors responsible for the increase in use of words from a specific region, such as an increase in the number of users from that location. However, another particularly influential factor is the growth of cultural interest from individuals outside the region. For instance, the growth of Korean food words is closely linked to the Korean Wave or *hallyu* phenomenon, with many words seeing an uptake in usage in English over the last decade. *Bibimbap* (비빔밥), a popular Korean rice dish, first entered into the third edition of the OED in 2011. Similarly, *soju* (소주, a type of spirit) and *doenjang* (된장, 'soybean paste') were added in 2017, with *gochujang* (고추장, 'hot-pepper paste') having also been added in 2016. In major English-language newspapers, Korean culinary terms like *japchae* (잡채), *bibimbap* (비빔밥), *pajeon* (파전), *kimbap* (김밥), *galbi* (갈비), and *bulgogi* (불고기) are appearing with increasing frequency. It is also noticeable that these terms have started to appear without special treatments, such as italicisation or capitalisation. In this way, we see how the spread of popular culture interest can also drive an expansion in food word usage.

4.2.4 Social media language use as cultural capital

Another important theme I want to propose in this book is the idea of social media language use as cultural capital, in line with Eckert's (2012) discussion of the 'third wave' of sociolinguistic theory. In this sense, style not only refers to a certain mode of pronunciation or register of speech, but also includes one's choice of words. That is to say that individual speakers choose words – beyond nation-state or linguistic borders – in order to situate themselves where they want to be in the social landscape. Furthermore, I argue that the availability of multiple words in the English language to express the same concept allows speakers a greater expressive range that serves to enhance lexical power and becomes cultural capital to the users (Hills, 2002).

As the use of language online is comparatively free and unregulated, social media serves as a sort of sanctuary for foreign words. While people have historically looked to dictionaries and lexicographers to adjudicate on what is and is not a valid English word, these judgements now have little influence over online platforms. There are simply too many words and too many variations in use on the Internet; lexicographers or linguistic authorities cannot easily detect them all. Instead, the general public is able to communicate transculturally, transnationally, and translingually anytime using their linguistic resources and conveying meanings in novel ways. In this way, social media liberates users from the rule-governed grammars and enables them to freely use various foreign-origin words as cultural capital.

Besides word choice, there are many examples of the use of grammatical variation as a type of cultural capital. Free from the constraints of official grammars, which seek to determine correct and incorrect usages of English, social media users are able to incorporate grammatical elements of other languages they know for stylistic effect. In this way, writings that would likely have been judged 'erroneous' if they appeared in print media are embraced as the embodiment of cultural capital by many in the social media community.

4.2.5 Amplification of minority cultures

A further effect of social media platforms like Twitter, Instagram, or Facebook is that they can make minority cultures more visible to a broad audience. Regardless of geographical location, individuals who share experiences with a particular minority culture are able to discuss these experiences online and build a sense of solidarity. For example, the following example refers to *ohaw*, a food word from the Ainu indigenous minority community of Northern Japan (Figure 4.6).

Traditional Ainu food differs considerably from the food associated with the majority ethnic Japanese group in Japan, in terms of both cooking methods and ingredients. Historically, it has been eclipsed by food culture of the much more numerous and politically dominant ethnic Japanese majority. Nonetheless, we see in the above example how social media allows individuals to share their experience with minority cultures and introduce their food words to a much broader audience. Perhaps more importantly, social media offers a platform for members of minority cultures themselves to communicate and share their food culture with others. In fact, members of minority cultures often use social media as a powerful tool to bring awareness to their foods and cooking methods, often intentionally targeting a global, English-speaking audience. Similarly, the following example discusses the food of Korean, Mongolian, and Tibetan minority groups in China (Figure 4.7).

Figure 4.6 Ainu cuisine on Twitter.

Global food words 85

Figure 4.7 Minority cuisines of China on Twitter.

Figure 4.8 Uighur cuisine on Twitter.

Likewise, foods originating in the culture of the Uighur Western ethnic minority have also attained popularity across the whole of modern China. A well-known example is *chong texse toxu qorumisi*, a type of chicken stew known as 大盘鸡 (*dàpánjī*) in Mandarin. Social media posts show the Chinese name for the dish has also spread outside of China, providing international exposure for a minority food culture (Figure 4.8).

4.2.6 Simplification of forms

A common feature of food words on social media is that forms are simplified for ease of communication and convenience. First, tone markers and diacritics are typically omitted in social media posts. A representative example is *bánh mì*, a type of Vietnamese sandwich, which is commonly presented as *banh mi* with the tones left unmarked. Similarly, the distinction between long and short vowels in Japanese is commonly not reflected in social media spellings. For example, the Japanese word for 'chilli pepper' 唐辛子 (*tōgarashi*), most accurately romanised with the use of a macron, is often rendered as *togarashi* with no macron. In cases where the poster has no knowledge of the original source language, they may not understand the significance of the diacritics, since they are rarely used in English, and thus regard the diacritic as redundant information. Furthermore, even if the social media user does understand the significance of the diacritic, they may have difficulty in typing it, as diacritic letters are rarely present on English keyboards. In combination, these factors produce a situation where word forms are simplified through the omission of 'special treatment' like tone markers and diacritics.

4.2.7 Variants of words

Global food words used on social media appear in multiple different forms and spellings, often with only subtle differences. Some of these variant forms are accidental, arising from the user's lack of proficiency in the food term's original source language. As social media content is not subject to approval by lexicographers, users are free to adopt and create new spellings as they wish. For example, the Korean dish *gimbap*, cooked rice and fillings wrapped in seaweed, was represented with various romanised spellings like *kimbab*, *kimbob*, and *kimbap*. Similarly, the example below shows an instance in which *bibimbap* has been referred to with the hashtag #bimbap (Figure 4.9).

Figure 4.9 Variant spelling of *bibimbap* on Twitter.

In the case of diverse spellings of *gimbap* or *bibimbap*, these variants all have more or less the same meaning. However, there are other instances where variants in word form have subtle differences in meaning. Through the creation of new food term variations with finely grained distinctions in meaning, social media users seek to achieve efficiency, expressivity, and empathy. To take an example, in the past, *ramen* and *ramyen* have been widely perceived as having the same meaning. *Ramyen* is a variant romanised spelling of the Korean term 라면 (*ramyeon*), which is also sometimes written as *ramyun*. A food word has been borrowed from Japanese into Korean and simply assimilated to the Korean sound system in the process. However, social media users have employed the borrowed form *ramyen* in their posts, reflecting the additional meaning that they are referring to a Korean form of the dish, rather than a Japanese version. Additionally, the term *ramyen* appeared to be associated with instant ramen rather than restaurant-cooked ramen. In this way, social media users are able to convey a large amount of additional information through a variant spelling. An example of *ramyen* word use on Twitter is presented below (Figure 4.10).

Figure 4.10 The finely grained distinction between *ramyen* and *ramen* on Twitter.

Another interesting example is that of *katsu* and *cutlet*. The Japanese word *katsu*, which is a shortened form of the longer *katsuretsu*, is transliterated from the English word *cutlet*. The English term *cutlet* is in turn derived from the French term *côtelette*, meaning 'meat chop'. On social media, there were multiple instances of the use of *katsu* even outside of a Japanese culinary context. For example, the figure below shows examples of how *katsu* has been employed in Mexican and German culinary contexts (Figure 4.11).

Even spellings based on the Korean borrowing of *katsu*, such as *donkasu*, were evidenced when the topic involved a Korean culinary context, as shown in Figure 4.12.

Sometimes, one single food word also shares multiple shades of meaning, such as the ambiguous term *bap*. *Bap* in the OED is defined as a small loaf or 'roll' of bakers' bread, made in various sizes and shapes in different parts of Scotland. However, in romanised Korean, *bap* also means cooked rice or, by extension, any food in general. In July 2019, searching on the hashtag #*bap* returned more results relating to Korean food than relating to bread rolls, even though it is the latter that is the recognised meaning in the OED. Furthermore, according to a Google search (10 July 2019), when the region is set based on Southeast Asia and Asia, *bap* was primarily understood as Korean rice. When the region is set based on US or UK, *bap* was primarily understood as a bread roll, but Korean rice was also ranked second among the possible meanings.

Figure 4.11 *Katsu* in international culinary contexts.

Figure 4.12 Korean *donkasu* on social media.

On social media, wide usage of the term *bokkeum* was also evidenced, originating from the Korean word for stir-frying. In the past, the term *bokkeum* was obscure in English and *stir-fry* was preferred. However, now the term is in common use online as part of the global English lexicon, appearing even in some non-Korean cuisine contexts. Although use of new terms like *bokkeum* may increase one's memory load, it can also be expressive and show empathy. The following examples show the use of *bokkeum* online (Figure 4.13).

Another case in which variant forms of food terms compete for usage on social media is that of calques or 'loan translations'. For instance, the Korean noodle dish *kalguksu* (칼국수) is regularly calqued as 'knife cut noodles'. Figure 4.14 shows how the romanised form and the calqued form are employed as variants on Twitter.

kalguksu
Knife-cut noodle

4.2.7.1 Dumpling:[19] translingual identity in social media

A prominent example of a food item with multiple variant names is the dumpling. A search on Google images produces results almost entirely comprised of Asian-style dumpling dishes. The term 'dumpling' has been adapted to all kinds of Asian cuisines and is used with a certain ubiquity. The term has come to generally describe any roughly

90 *Global food words*

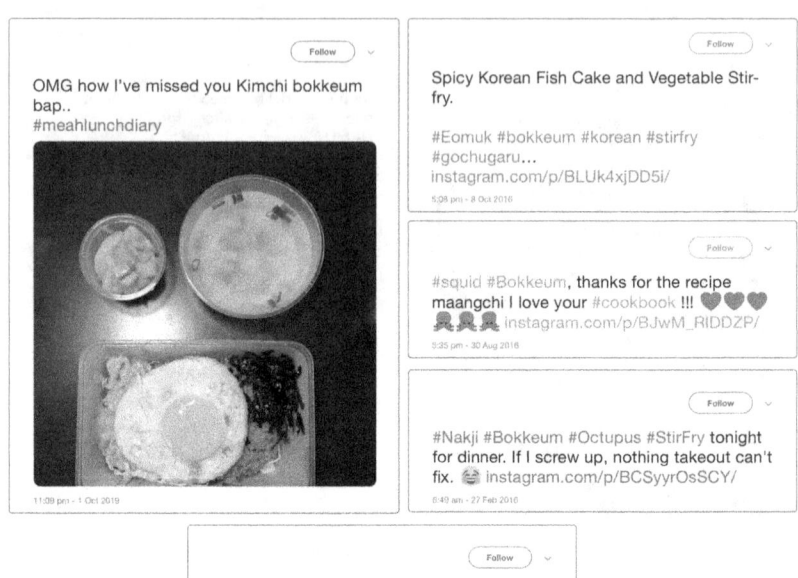

Figure 4.13 Bokkeum on Twitter.

rounded dough-based item, either containing another filling or empty, cooked in almost any method (the most popular being steaming, boiling, and frying). While homogeneously terming items that are labelled with entirely different names in their original languages – such as describing Chinese *bāozi* (steamed buns) and *shuǐjiǎo* (boiled dumplings) with the same name – the word has also come to cover all manner of hybridisations and Westernised dishes. An initial search for dumpling recipes online results in a wealth of hybrid dishes including 'bacon

Global food words 91

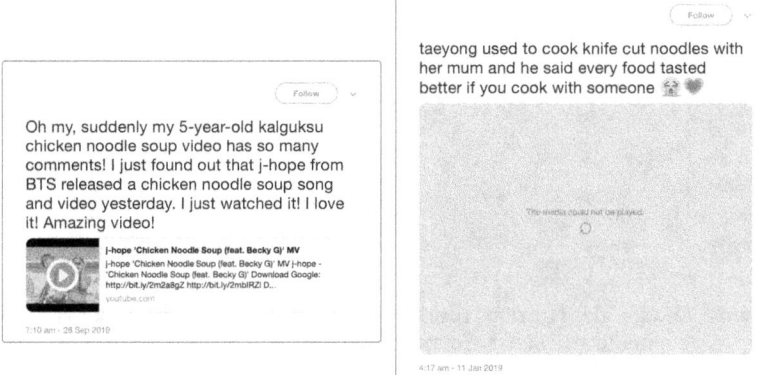

Figure 4.14 Calqued term 'knife cut noodles' on Twitter.

cheeseburger dumplings', 'Mom's special vegan dumplings', and 'Asian vegetable dumplings'. Dishes such as these offer two key insights: first, that we are so comfortable with the term *dumpling* that we see fit to adapt it to our own tastes; and second, that using one term for a variety of distinct East Asian dishes has led to their homogenisation or 'Pan-Asianisation'. This can be seen in the wealth of online recipes described as 'Asian style x' or 'Oriental y', indicating how our adaptation of English-language terms to describe dishes has exacerbated a lack of awareness with regard to the distinct nature of these cuisines.

I have taken the three items – Japanese *gyoza*, Chinese *jiaozi*, and Korean *mandu* – as examples of the most representative 'dumpling' item in each cuisine. While these transliterated terms have a solid position in the English lexicon, with the terms *jiaozi* and *gyoza* entering the OED in 1965 and 1978 respectively (with the exact same definition other than country of origin), a comparison in both online searches and published works demonstrated the overwhelming popularity maintained by the use of the English-language term *dumpling*. An upward trend in searches for the transliterated terms, in particular *gyoza* and *jiaozi*, online over recent years may, however, demonstrate how social media has caused an increase in our awareness of native terms for dumpling dishes (Figure 4.15).

It can also clearly be seen that the Japanese term *gyoza* and the Chinese term *jiaozi* differ in popularity throughout all searches, despite being written using the same characters (饺子), deriving from the same originally Chinese dish, and having the same official

Figure 4.15 Google N-gram results for 'dumpling', 'gyoza', 'jiaozi', and 'mandu', English Corpus, 1800–2000.

definition in the English language. The consistently higher use of the Japanese term, alongside its earlier official entry into the English lexicon, is a reflection of greater awareness of Japanese foods and their names in English-speaking world. This is most likely a reflection of the longer history of connection between post-war Japan and the English-speaking West, as well as the perceived accessibility of Japan linguistically, culturally, and politically, compared to China. Differing from eaters in Japan, most of whom recognise their *gyoza* dishes to have originated in China, eaters in the English-speaking West seem more likely to be aware of the Japanese transliterated term than the original Chinese.

The dominance of the Japanese language in labelling Pan-Asian concepts can be seen in a survey of related posts on social media. While many posts on both Twitter and Instagram feature the hashtag #*gyoza* without further explanation, the far less popular hashtags #*jiaozi* and #*guotie* (Chinese pan-fried dumplings) are used most often in combination with the word *dumpling* or other varieties of Asian dumpling-like foods by means of explanation, as shown in the following tweets (Figures 4.16 and 4.17).

The first tweet is an example of someone describing a Chinese-style dumpling dish *guotie* using the qualifying terms *jiaozi*, potstickers, *gyoza*, and dumplings, as the Chinese transliterated name alone is not considered enough to make it clear to the average English speaker what the dish is. The second tweet also demonstrates this, with the term *jiaozi* being put in brackets between the words *dumpling* and *wonton*, as these are clearly perceived to be more commonly recognisable terms to English speakers.

Figure 4.16 #*guotie* on Twitter.

Figure 4.17 #*jiaozi* on Twitter.

94 *Global food words*

Figure 4.18 Instagram results for Jamaican #dumplings.

A search for #dumplings on Instagram also serves to prove the flexibility of the term and the incredible breadth of cuisines it covers. Posts tagged #dumplings include Chinese *jiaozi*, *guotie*, and *sheng jian bao*; Hong Kong *cha siu bao* and *har gow*; Japanese *gyoza*; Korean *mandu*; Polish *pierogi*; Jamaican fried and steamed dumplings; and Anglo-American sweet and savoury suet dumplings (Figure 4.18).

It is interesting to note that while 'dumpling'-like dishes of almost any culture can be termed as such in the English language, it is only Italian dumpling-like dishes that are rarely referred to as 'dumplings', with very few posts featuring dumpling-like pastas such as ravioli, gnocchi, or tortellini cropping up in social media and Google searches for the word. Indeed, we can also note that, in British English more so than US, non-stuffed Italian pastas are not homogenised under the term 'noodle' as are all Asian varieties of what is effectively the same item. This could be considered to be a product of Britain's longer history with and greater awareness of Italian culture, as well as the perceived authenticity of Italian food names. Where there are a host of Asian foods homogenised under English-language terms such as *dumplings* or *noodles*, the principal terms for Italian foods remain in the original language (such as *pasta* and *pizza*). This demonstrates our increased willingness to give generic labels to less familiar global cuisines, opting instead to use adapted terms from our own language that we are already comfortable with.

Having seen the varieties of international 'dumplings' in existence, we return to the very clear fact that the term has been wholeheartedly overtaken by East Asian varieties of the dish, almost totally losing its original meaning of Euro-American style steamed or baked puddings. A search of English-language publications reveals that the term *dumpling* was used almost exclusively in reference to Anglo-American style apple or suet dumplings until the late-nineteenth century. Even in the mid-twentieth century, when Asian dumplings seem to have become more common in literature, requiring no subsequent explanation as to what they refer to, cookbooks and recipes still seemed to be only for British-, American-, and German-style dumpling dishes. This suggests the adaptation of the term to almost solely refer to Asian dishes is a far more recent phenomenon. The popularity of the word *dumpling* in English-language publications fluctuates, reaching one high in the mid-1800s, dipping during the mid-twentieth century, and then picking up again towards the end of the century on a sharp incline towards a new high at the start of the twenty-first century. I suggest that these two peaks in the graph (see Figure 4.19) represent the two high points of popularity for 'dumplings' in their two different meanings: the first being of the traditional Anglo-American variety, and the second representing the growing popularity of 'Asian' dumplings since the late twentieth century.

4.2.7.2 Bubble tea: how forms and meanings of words are negotiated in social media

Bubble tea is a beverage which is popular in East Asia and has exploded in popularity in recent years in the West. Bubble tea can refer to various flavours of tea, usually combined with milk, which can also have different toppings such as tapioca pearls, pudding, or jelly. This iteration of the beverage originated in Taiwan, and can now be found across East Asia. In Mandarin Chinese, bubble tea is called 奶茶 *nǎichá* for various flavours of milk tea, and 珍珠奶茶 *zhēnzhū nǎichá* for milk tea with tapioca pearls. However, in English there are various names for this beverage including bubble tea, where the word

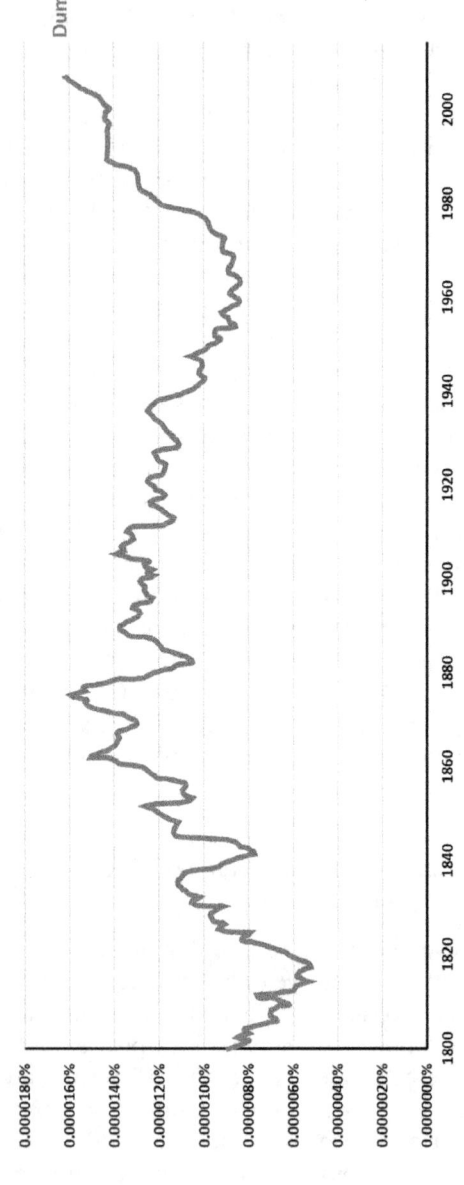

Figure 4.19 Google N-gram results for 'dumpling', English corpus, 1500–2008.

'bubble' originated in reference to the bubbles created when the drink is shaken; boba (tea), where boba refers to a slang term 波霸 *bōbà* meaning 'big breasts' which refers to the tapioca pearls; and (pearl) milk tea, the calqued form of (*zhēnzhū*) *nǎichá* (珍珠)奶茶.[20] These terms are contested on English-language social media. In the USA, an East-West divide has been noted in the use of the terms bubble tea and boba tea.[21] The examples below are from the Facebook group Subtle Asian Traits, and show the active way in which these English terms are negotiated on social media (Figure 4.20).

The first user calls the use of the term 'boba' to refer to both the beverage and the tapioca pearls a 'linguistical trainwreck'; another user responds that attempts to police use of terminology is "nothing more than linguistic gaslighting by elitist prescriptivists" and argues that the term 'boba' is 'culturally significant' to Asian Americans. From the tone of the posts, which use argumentative but hyperbolic language, it appears that the debate is intended to be seen as playful. Nevertheless, these online debates show the ways in which variants of food terms appear and come into contact with each other on social media. By discussing and debating these terms and their usage, social media users from different geographical locations are actively engaged in negotiating the forms, meanings, and identities of global food words.

The posts say that the term 'boba' is not used in China or Taiwan; however, comments contradict this statement. Nevertheless, the second poster (Figure 4.21) claims that boba is a term which is 'culturally significant' to Asian Americans, whether it has a legitimate

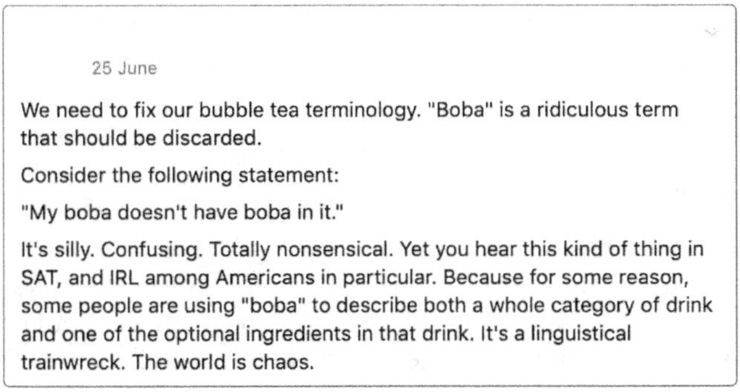

---

25 June

We need to fix our bubble tea terminology. "Boba" is a ridiculous term that should be discarded.

Consider the following statement:

"My boba doesn't have boba in it."

It's silly. Confusing. Totally nonsensical. Yet you hear this kind of thing in SAT, and IRL among Americans in particular. Because for some reason, some people are using "boba" to describe both a whole category of drink and one of the optional ingredients in that drink. It's a linguistical trainwreck. The world is chaos.

Figure 4.20 Post from the Facebook group Subtle Asian Traits debating terms for 'bubble tea'.[22]

98 *Global food words*

> 26 June
>
> Our boba terminology is fine. "Boba" as a term is fine, and any attempt to claim otherwise is nothing more than linguistic gaslighting by elitist prescriptivists.

> "Boba" is culturally significant. It may be true that the term was not used in China or Taiwan, but Asian Americans have adopted boba as a part of their own unique culture. Within the context of Asian American culture, there is no denying the significance of "boba".

Figure 4.21 Post from the Facebook group Subtle Asian Traits debating terms for 'bubble tea'.[23]

linguistic root in East Asia or not. This shows how the Asian diaspora negotiates and understands translingual meanings and identity through reference to the languages of their cultural heritage, but also holds space for their own diaspora identities and vocabularies which are developed partially on social media. The original post amassed 26,000 reactions and 11,000 comments[24] and the response has gained 5,600 reactions and 2,700 comments to date.[25] The astonishing level of engagement with these posts shows the power of social media in allowing global food terms and word variants to thrive, and to create conversation, including the negotiation of cultural meanings. In this example, social media has encouraged those with Asian heritage to engage with their cultural and linguistic heritage through the popularisation of, and debate surrounding, English language terms for East Asian food and beverage terms; but has also provided a space for them to create and debate new terms. Furthermore, while these terms are claimed as being significant to Asian diaspora communities, they are also used much more broadly, and have a global identity.

4.3 Food word transmission and education through vlogging

In recent years, blogs and vlogs (video blogs) have become an important platform through which social media users introduce and discuss recipes and food terms from across the world. In particular, recipe videos on YouTube have become extremely popular. Jocuns writes that YouTube videos "follow a similar pattern to the initiation-response-follow-up, IRF, framework often found in classroom interaction, which has been extended to use in everyday English conversation"

(Jocuns, 2018: 43). For this reason, YouTube videos are suitable for language and intercultural learning, and may offer opportunities for mutual cross-cultural language development. In the context of food words, this means that through watching vloggers' recipe videos on YouTube, viewers can learn about foods and food terms from different languages and cultures; and by interacting with viewers, vloggers themselves are also involved in the creation and transmission of food terms for a potentially global audience.

4.3.1 Case study: 'Asian Auntie' food vloggers

According to Seargeant and Tagg (2014), the concept of authenticity is essential to online communication, and social value is placed on perceived authenticity. Authenticity also fosters trust, and is generally a buzz word in recent food trends. Therefore, vloggers who are perceived to have authentic knowledge of the food cultures they are discussing may be more popular on platforms such as YouTube. One popular Korean food vlogger goes by the name of Maangchi. She produces recipe videos and runs a blog in English, and has over a million subscribers on YouTube, as of October 2019.[26] Maangchi is quoted saying: "the Korean recipes I saw in English were full of mistakes, and I wanted to show the real way we do things".[27] In this way, content creators such as Maangchi are perceived as trustworthy sources of 'authentic' Asian recipes. Seid writes that "Asian auntie cooking web series engage social media and online fandoms in ways that assert Asian American women's identities within food media and a foodie culture largely dominated by male hipster chefs" (Seid, 2018: 779). This allows Asian women to "simultaneously pass on cooking knowledge and question assumptions about cultural authority" (Seid, 2018: 780). In this way, the 'Asian Auntie' figure can be seen as a challenge to the history of Asian food and food terms being homogenised, simplified, or Westernised through language. Maangchi notes that she has to do things the right way or she "will hear about it from the Koreans".[28] This push back against Pan-Asianisation by authentic gatekeepers of food heritage is facilitated by social media platforms, which allow them to share their authentic knowledge and food terms directly with viewers around the world, offering a direct pathway for local words to become globally recognised terms in World Englishes.

Jocuns notes how the use of language by vloggers such as Maangchi evolves over time, writing that "earlier, her language was not that nuanced, however, later, she used more complex linguistic practices such as anthropomorphisation and reduplication" (Jocuns, 2018: 44). In this way, vloggers – whose first language may not be English – develop their own style within the English language which shows their personality and endears them to their audience, while also transmitting authentic food knowledge and language from their culture. In other words, through vlogging about Korean food, Maangchi has not only developed a cute and humorous personal style of communication in English, but has also educated viewers on Korean cooking styles, introduced Korean food terms, and "school[ed] her viewers in the proper pronunciation of dishes".[29] In this way, authentic Korean terms and pronunciations are transmitted to English speakers while situated within an English language context. This may mean that new terms are therefore absorbed directly into viewers' English language vocabulary, despite being purely Korean terms.

Diaspora YouTubers also play a part in this process. Language acquisition among members of the diaspora varies widely, but their linguistic flexibility and engagement with both East Asian and Western cultures means that they are well placed to create content which can bridge any gaps in understanding. Ethnically Korean YouTubers in the diaspora can therefore introduce predominantly English-speaking audiences to Korean words – often through food – in a way that may be more easily relatable.[30] The transmission of food words through vlogging cultures is also exemplified by the popularity of the *mukbang* format in which vloggers consume a large quantity of food for an audience. The *mukbang* phenomenon originated on Korean social media, but nowadays English-speaking YouTubers also brand their videos as 'mukbangs'.

As more monolingual English speakers begin to learn East Asian languages, they too are playing a role in transmitting cultural and linguistic knowledge. For example, the YouTube channel Korean Englishman (영국남자, *Yeongungnamja*) is primarily hosted by two British English speakers, one of whom has learned Korean as a second language. Their content presents information in both Korean and English, with the language not being spoken translated in subtitles. Their videos are a truly bilingual experience, which is accessible even for monolinguals. This is reflected in the comment section of their videos which, rather than being dominated by English-language comments, displays a strong proportion of Korean-language interaction. Many of their videos are about eating and food culture in Korea. Related side channels show additional recipes and taste tests. The majority of their food videos are filmed in restaurants in Korea, locating the experience of eating Korean cuisine within its original linguistic and cultural context. As their Korean audience has grown, Korean

Englishman has also begun to introduce British cultural and linguistic phenomena through their channel.

4.3.2 Case study: use of subtitles by Chinese vloggers

In addition to the Asian-American food vloggers discussed above who communicate with their audience in spoken English and teach individual terms in target languages, many Chinese food vloggers communicate with English-speaking audiences in a different way: through subtitles. One example is Ms Yeah who, as of December 2019, has eight million subscribers on YouTube and posts humorous videos about cooking in her office.[31] A very different example is Li Ziqi who, as of December 2019, has 21.6 million followers on Weibo and 7.7 million subscribers on YouTube.[32] Li Ziqi produces high-quality videos which show her making Chinese food the old fashioned way in rural China, often showing scenes of her foraging for ingredients in the natural landscape. Both vloggers produce content which is mostly dialogue-free, but which offers English subtitles for food terms and some conversational elements. This encourages the audience to negotiate meaning and create language associations or do research for themselves, as unfamiliar terms are translated but not explained any further.

Nevertheless, even without a spoken English element, a lot of cultural knowledge is transferred through these videos. For example, in one of Ms Yeah's videos, a humorous exchange between office workers explains regional differences in Chinese cuisine as her colleagues debate the proper filling for *siu mai* dumplings.[33] While conversation is often not translated in Li Ziqi's videos, there are humorous cautions presenting in English, such as "careful when replicating this at home. We don't want fermented finger tips and nails".[34] In this way, Chinese vloggers communicate with English-speaking viewers through written subtitles and humorous annotations, rather than by speaking English. This shows the ways in which the multimodal characteristics of social media communication can assist in allowing food terms to cross over more easily between languages and cultures and gain global recognition.

However, despite the desire to reach foreign fans, the content being produced does not pander to a foreign, English-speaking audience. The videos are created primarily with a Chinese-speaking audience in mind. Therefore, other than providing subtitles, Ms Yeah and Li Ziqi leave it up to the audience to look up terms they do not understand, or wish to know more about. Nonetheless, view counts for their videos are in the millions. As these videos are mostly dialogue-free and focused on the visual elements, viewers are not overwhelmed by audio they do not understand, and can still gain understanding through non-verbal forms of communication, such as visual representations. However, the subtitles offer an entry point for those interested in learning more about the Chinese language, although they cannot directly assist in teaching pronunciation. The fact that these videos are presented in the original language associated with the recipes may also contribute to a sense of authenticity, and challenge the homogenisation of Asian food terms in English.

4.4 Summary

Due to globalisation and diverse means and areas of language contact, notably social media, first- and second-generation English terms for East Asian foods and beverages are gaining global recognition, often entering other languages in their anglicised forms, rather than undergoing a new process of transliteration. This is further facilitated by the prevalence of English as a global lingua franca. These global words have complex origins, which are sometimes masked by their anglicised form, but also demonstrate fluidity as their forms, meanings, and identities continue to develop and be actively debated, primarily in an online setting. The definitions and usages of these words are rarely adjudicated by linguistic authorities, but are mediated and negotiated through global discourse.

Notes

1. www.census.gov/library/publications/2013/acs/acs-22.html.
2. www12.statcan.gc.ca/census-recensement/2011/as-sa/98-314-x/98-314-x2011001-eng.cfm.
3. www.bbc.com/news/business-44770777.
4. www.telegraph.co.uk/education/2018/08/16/chinese-a-level-overtakes-german-first-time-becoming-uks-third/.
5. www.duolingo.com/courses.
6. https://web.archive.org/web/20180327132827/http://www.moj.go.jp/content/001254624.pdf.
7. www.immigration.gov.tw/5475/5478/141478/141380/198503/.
8. www.koreaherald.com/view.php?ud=20161006000812.
9. www.koreatimes.co.kr/www/nation/2019/03/181_265235.html.
10. www.koreaherald.com/view.php?ud=20180925000067.
11. www.abc.net.au/news/2012-09-13/herscovitch-english-asia/4257442.
12. www.uni-due.de/ELE/Spread_of_English_(Asia).pdf.
13. www.abc.net.au/news/2012-09-13/herscovitch-english-asia/4257442.

14 www.theguardian.com/news/2019/jul/01/global-tourism-hits-record-highs-but-who-goes-where-on-holiday.
15 www.e-unwto.org/doi/pdf/10.18111/9789284421152 (accessed 22nd December 2019).
16 www.theguardian.com/news/2019/jul/01/global-tourism-hits-record-highs-but-who-goes-where-on-holiday.
17 www.theguardian.com/news/2019/jul/01/global-tourism-hits-record-highs-but-who-goes-where-on-holiday.
18 Image via Emojipedia Galaxy Emoji List: https://emojipedia.org/samsung/.
19 Thanks to Niamh Calway for the data collection and insights.
20 www.bubbleteaology.com/boba-bubble-tea/.
21 https://nextshark.com/boba-bubble-tea-tapioca/.
22 www.facebook.com/groups/1343933772408499/permalink/1874736932661511/.
23 www.facebook.com/groups/1343933772408499/permalink/1897710890364115/.
24 www.facebook.com/groups/1343933772408499/permalink/1874736932661511/.
25 www.facebook.com/groups/1343933772408499/permalink/1897710890364115/.
26 www.maangchi.com/1million.
27 www.nytimes.com/2015/06/03/dining/maangchi-youtube-korean-julia-child.html (accessed 12 October 2019).
28 www.nytimes.com/2015/06/03/dining/maangchi-youtube-korean-julia-child.html.
29 www.nytimes.com/2015/06/03/dining/maangchi-youtube-korean-julia-child.html.
30 For example, Jenn Im, oh no nina, and Stephanie Soo.
31 www.youtube.com/channel/UCRB4xZ_2ew7fzmrcv8aj4Lw (accessed 22nd December 2019).
32 See https://weibo.com/mianyangdanshen?refer_flag=1005055014_ and www.youtube.com/channel/UCoC47do520os_4DBMEFGg4A (accessed 22nd December 2019).
33 www.youtube.com/watch?v=CUZ0VSCjzVU (accessed 22nd December 2019).
34 www.youtube.com/watch?v=_jUJrIWp2I4 (accessed 22nd December 2019).

5 New words as cultural capital

In this chapter, I discuss how global food words are used as cultural capital across the world, with a particular focus on the relationship between East Asia and the West. I explore how English words of East Asian origin are used in English languages, and also how English is used as cultural capital in East Asia. Throughout this discussion, I seek to link cultural capital to the phenomenon of foreign branding. In the first section of the chapter, I introduce the idea of cultural capital, before explaining the concept's relevance to foreign branding practices. From there, I discuss Western companies' use of branding in East Asian markets. Subsequently, I explore how East Asian companies opt to present their products overseas. I then outline, with examples, how foreign branding incorporating English words is used as cultural capital by East Asian corporations targeting even domestic consumers. Moving on to discuss the situation in the Western Europe, I introduce examples of the use of Asian words as foreign branding by domestic companies.

5.1 Cultural capital

The idea of 'cultural capital' was first posited by Pierre Bourdieu in the 1980s as a description of "the symbols, tastes, and preferences that can be strategically used as resources in social action". It is regularly compared to the long-standing idea of economic capital, with both variants of capital able to be accumulated, invested, or converted.[1] By investing or converting their cultural capital, individuals are able to exploit these resources to help them attain success in society. While the term 'cultural capital' first appeared in sociology, it also has implications for the field of linguistics and beyond. Indeed, Bourdieu described 'linguistic capital' as a subtype of cultural capital, referring to speakers' communication skills, which are influential in

New words as cultural capital 105

determining their social status. For example, a use of linguistic capital might be an individual skilfully applying politeness registers in order to persuade others to reward them with advancement at university or in a work setting.

Across East Asia, the ability to speak English is one important type of linguistic cultural capital. For example, in Japan, demonstrating knowledge of English is an important factor in securing employment at the most socially prestigious, highest-paying companies. Accordingly, job applicants may take formal English proficiency examinations like TOEIC multiple times in order to boost the score they can write on their resume. In this way, some job searchers try to outdo rival applicants in numeric measures of their English level in an attempt to boost their social position. Similarly, in South Korea, many parents seek to convert their economic capital into linguistic capital for their children, spending large sums on private English education. In this way, English competency is seen as a vital determinant of social success in many East Asian countries, where it has come to constitute cultural capital.

5.2 Cultural capital by association

For businesses and their employees, an important area of application for linguistic cultural capital is marketing. In order to attain commercial success, it is important that businesses are able to find and maintain buyers for their products. The sound application of communication skills is an important aspect of satisfying customers, and a crucial skill for marketers.

Under the umbrella of marketing, this chapter focuses specifically on the field of branding. According to the Cambridge Business English Dictionary, branding is "the activity of connecting a product with a particular name, symbol, etc. or with particular features or ideas, in order to make people recognize and want to buy it".[2] Language is a crucial tool as marketers seek to associate their product with ideas and names, providing an opportunity to apply linguistic cultural capital.

Branding that incorporates elements from foreign languages or cultures, such as incorporating words or a writing system from another country, is commonly known as 'foreign branding'. In the twenty-first century, increased global commerce and trade in our super-diverse, multilingual society has made foreign branding extremely popular. Foreign branding sometimes occurs when corporations become multinational, expanding beyond the market of their Country-Of-Origin (COO). Well-known East Asian companies that use foreign words in their branding in the English-speaking world include *Hyundai* (meaning 'modern' in Korean) and *Huawei* (meaning 'China shows promise' in Mandarin). Furthermore, some product names are quickly and widely earning the status of common, global words in our time. To illustrate, in the Japanese language, the corporate brand name *Google* is now in common use not only as a noun but also as a verb ググる (*guguru*, 'to search for information using a search engine'),[3] in parallel with the use of the verb 'to google' in English.[4] Similarly, the global word 'Android' has entered East Asian languages in recent years to describe a type of smartphone. Terms for the brand 'Android' are distinct from local words meaning 'android' as in robotics. The branding term is usually a transliteration of the original English brand name, for example *Ānzhuō* (安卓) in Mandarin, while the robotics term is a translation of the meaning of *Android*, for example, *jīqìrén* (机器人, lit. 'mechanical person') in Mandarin. While not yet listed in the Oxford English Dictionary (OED), the scope and frequency of use of *Android* demonstrates its position as a global English word.

Companies have also used foreign branding to target customers in the domestic market of their own country. Research on the importance of perceived Country-Of-Origin (COO) has provided some empirical support for the effectiveness of foreign branding within a wholly domestic context. A 2011 study showed evidence that perceived country of origin influences customer attitudes based on their preconceptions of that country, supporting the conclusions of much previous research in the area. However, the study also confirmed that consumers often perceive COO incorrectly, assuming a product comes from a different place than its actual origin (Magnusson, Westjohn, and Zdravkovic, 2011). In this way, from a marketing perspective, customer's perceived COO could be seen as more important than the objectively true COO. These findings may account, to some extent, for the phenomenon of companies using foreign branding to target domestic markets: by encouraging the false belief among customers that the product is foreign, companies can make use of customers' positive image of the perceived COO.

A prominent example of foreign branding in the UK is provided by the popular sandwich chain *Pret a Manger*, which based its brand name on the French phrase 'Prêt à Manger', meaning 'ready to eat', despite the fact that the chain was founded in the UK in 1986 to serve a domestic market. *Pret a Manger* did not open any international stores until the year 2000, and does not have a particularly French-themed menu.[5] In this case, it appears that the name was chosen because of perceived positive connotations of French cuisine among British consumers, perhaps playing on France's international fame for haute cuisine, rather than a need to communicate with Francophone customers. The company's marketers have applied linguistic cultural capital through their choice of language for their brand name, thereby increasing the attractiveness of the chain to potential customers. Another example is the Casual Dining Group which operates a number of restaurants in the UK, many of which incorporate foreign branding in their names. For example, Bella Italia, Café Rouge, and La Tasca.

Most research on foreign branding is conducted from the perspective of marketing rather than taking a linguistic focus. In particular, there is scope for more work on the multilingual reality of a globalised East Asia, and the growth of hybrid branding utilising both local languages and English. In this chapter, I discuss the application of cultural capital to the process of foreign branding in East Asia and the West. To begin with, in the next section, I discuss the foreign branding of Western companies in East Asian markets.

5.3 Western companies' foreign branding in East Asia

A number of different strategies have been used to present foreign brand names to East Asian audiences. First, some brands simply present their name in the original alphabet, without any explicit localisation. A prominent example is the American beverage company Coca-Cola, which uses its original Roman alphabet logo on its eponymous soft drink product in Japan. The Roman alphabet is already used widely in Japan due to globalisation, even though it is not a native writing system of the country. As a result, it is not an obstacle to consumers' understanding to present the original brand name. Additionally, it is perhaps the case that, since the brand is so widely known across the world, the logo is instantly recognisable to most people anyway, regardless of the writing system used (Figure 5.1).

Figure 5.1 Coca-Cola can in Kobe, Japan.

An additional option is for the company to transliterate their name into the writing system of the local language. For example, the fast food chain *McDonald's* markets itself in Japan as マクドナルドハンバーガー (*makudonarudo hanbāgā*) (Figure 5.2).

Another prominent example is the American processed meat product *Spam*, which is highly popular in South Korea. In South Korea, *Spam* has an image as a luxury food product and is sometimes presented as a gift during the annual lunar harvest festival *Chuseok* (추석).[6] The image below shows a *Spam* gift hamper on sale ahead of *Chuseok* in South Korea, with the brand name transliterated into Korean as 스팸 (*Seupaem*) on the packaging (Figure 5.3).

Sometimes the brand name is presented in the original writing system alongside a transliteration, with both being used in marketing materials and signage. Figure 5.4 shows a *Pizza Hut* delivery moped in Japan, branded with the name both in Roman letters, and in the Japanese transliteration ピザハット (*pizahatto*).

Similarly, in the case of the fast food outlet *Burger King* in South Korea, the original English name and the transliteration 버거킹 (*Beogeoking*) are both used. Compared to presenting only the original name in the Roman alphabet, also providing a transliteration is likely to help customers to remember the brand, especially for consumers with lower English reading proficiency. In this way, we see how marketing professionals in these food companies have applied their linguistic cultural capital to make their products more memorable and to attain greater commercial success.

Figure 5.2 McDonald's (マクドナルドハンバーガー, *makudonarudo hanbāgā*) restaurant in Tokyo, Japan.

New words as cultural capital 109

Figure 5.3 Spam (스팸, *Seupaem*) gift set on sale in Busan, South Korea.

Figure 5.4 Pizza Hut (ピザハット, *pizahatto*) delivery moped in Kobe, Japan.

In South Korea, the alphabetic system 한글 *Hangeul* is used to transliterate foreign-origin words and, in Japan, the syllabic system カタカナ *Katakana* is normally employed. In contrast, in the case of the Chinese language, there is no equivalent native syllabary or alphabet in use. Instead, Chinese characters (汉字 *hànzì*) are used for transliterations. As each *hànzì* grapheme is associated not only with sound but also with logographic meaning, the characters of a brand name may give rise to connotations in the mind of the consumer. Some transliterations of common brand names into Chinese are relatively faithful to the original pronunciation, and generally do not reflect a coherent meaning. For example, the Chinese characters of the name of the fruit-flavoured soft drink *Fanta* (芬达 *fēndá*) might be translated as 'fragrance arrival'. Similarly, the Chinese name for *Dove* chocolate (marketed as *Galaxy* in countries like the UK) is 德芙 *défú*, or 'morality hibiscus'.

However, many foreign businesses in China, in the process of transliterating their brand name, select characters for their positive connotations rather than faithfulness to the sounds of the original name. To take an example, the official Chinese transliteration of the American chocolate brand *Hershey's* is 好时 *hǎo shí*. While it would be possible to approximate the pronunciation of *Hershey's* more closely, the official transliteration holds the additional advantage of meaning 'good times' in Chinese, immediately conveying positive connotations to the consumer. Similarly, *Pepsi Cola*'s Chinese transliteration is 百事可乐 *bǎishì kělè*, which can be interpreted as 'everything is delightful' or 'a hundred things are happy'. These examples demonstrate marketers' ingenuity in applying their linguistic cultural capital, using their knowledge of Chinese characters to select a transliteration that conveys a positive image to their customers.

Another strategy, also more commonly seen in China than in Japan or South Korea, is the calquing of the original brand name. In this case, the localised brand name is chosen for its closeness to the meaning of the original, rather than for closeness in sound. A prominent example is the energy drink *Red Bull*, which is referred to in China as 红牛 *hóngniú*, literally meaning 'red bull'. While the Chinese name bares no relation to the English pronunciation whatsoever, the name does have the advantage of being short and snappy; a transliteration of *Red Bull* into standard Mandarin would likely require more than two characters. By opting for a short, memorable name, the brand has exploited its linguistic capital to increase potential revenue from product consumers (Figure 5.5).

Some companies opt for a combination method, transliterating some parts of their name and translating other parts. A representative household name is 星巴克咖啡 *xīng bākè kāfēi*, the Chinese name for the *Starbucks Coffee* chain. In this name, the first character 星 *xīng* literally means 'star' and is thus a translation of the first component of the English brand name. The 'bucks' and 'coffee' are both represented by transliterations of the English. However, *kāfēi*, the transliteration of 'coffee', has successfully entered and been accepted as part of the Chinese vocabulary and is used beyond the *Starbucks* brand, whereas

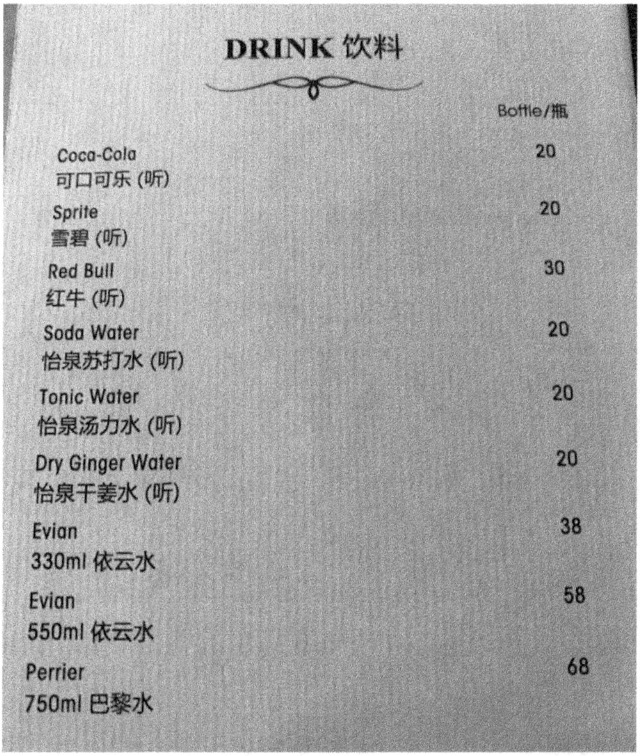

DRINK 饮料

	Bottle/瓶
Coca-Cola 可口可乐 (听)	20
Sprite 雪碧 (听)	20
Red Bull 红牛 (听)	30
Soda Water 怡泉苏打水 (听)	20
Tonic Water 怡泉汤力水 (听)	20
Dry Ginger Water 怡泉干姜水 (听)	20
Evian 330ml 依云水	38
Evian 550ml 依云水	58
Perrier 750ml 巴黎水	68

Figure 5.5 Drinks menu featuring Red Bull (红牛, *hóngniú*) in Shanghai, China.

bākè is a transliteration purely for branding purposes that holds no meaning in broader language use. This makes *Starbucks Coffee* a particularly interesting example, as it includes translation, use of accepted transliterations which have entered general vocabulary, and individual transliterations for branding purposes. In this way, the name 星巴克咖啡 *xīng bākè kāfēi* contains the expressive term 'star' which evokes a positive image, the foreign term 'bucks' which highlights the brand's foreign COO, and the efficient term 'coffee' which directly tells consumers what products they can expect to find in-store (Figure 5.6).

Returning to the previous example of *Burger King*, the Chinese name for this chain is 汉堡王 *hànbǎo wáng*. In this brand name, the first two characters, 汉堡 *hànbǎo*, are a transliteration of the English word 'hamburger', which is now commonly used in contemporary

112 *New words as cultural capital*

Figure 5.6 Starbucks Coffee (星巴克咖啡 *xīng bākè kāfēi*) shop in Shanghai, China.

China. However, the third character, 王 *wáng*, literally means 'king' and is not intended to transliterate English. In this way, the Chinese word for *Burger King* might also be seen as a mix of transliteration and translation (Figure 5.7).

Finally, some Western brands in East Asia abandon outright the idea of presenting their existing brand name to an Asian audience. Instead, these companies create a totally new brand name in the local language that bears no relation to the original in terms of either meaning or sound. A prominent example is the beer corporation *Heineken*, which is known as 喜力 *Xǐlì* in China. *Xǐlì* is clearly not a transliteration, nor is it a translation of the Dutch family name Heineken; rather, it means something along the lines of 'joy and strength'. In this case, it appears that a totally new Chinese brand name has been selected for the positive connotations of its characters, rather than attempting to transpose the original name. Other companies choose to translate some elements of their name, and replace other elements. To illustrate, the soft drink *7 up* is called 七喜 *qī xǐ* in China. In this Chinese name, the first character 七 *qī* means '7' and does reflect the original brand, but the second part 喜 *xǐ* means 'joy' rather than 'up'. In this way, the

New words as cultural capital 113

Figure 5.7 Burger King (漢堡王, *hànbǎo wáng*) shop in Hsinchu, Taiwan.

English and Chinese versions of the brand name are totally divergent in sound but only partially divergent in meaning.

As demonstrated by the case studies above, different Western companies take different decisions on how to present their products to an East Asian audience. Decisions regarding transliteration, translation, or the adoption of an entirely new brand name are highly dependent on the nature of the product itself, and of the target market. Important considerations are likely to include: the COO, the target country, the age and education level of the target demographic, the meanings of the original brand name, and so on. To take one example, in 2002, an investigation was conducted to examine the case of brands with Roman-alphabetic names seeking to present their product to Mandarin Chinese speakers. Based on experimental evidence of Singaporean consumers' reception of fruit juices, the study concluded that a transcription in Chinese characters may be mandatory for an unknown brand. However, companies with an existing, strong brand name would be well advised to maintain their original brand in Roman letters with no transcription. The findings also suggested that, in practice, it is sensible to provide the name both in Roman letters and in

114 *New words as cultural capital*

transliteration on the product (Hong, Pecotich, and Shultz, 2002). As these findings examined a specific scenario of Mandarin speakers' reception of fruit juice, they cannot necessarily be generalised to extend to Western audiences, or indeed to other contexts in East Asia. The diversity of different factors influencing foreign branding decisions explains the range of different approaches introduced above.

5.4 East Asian companies' foreign branding for international markets

East Asian companies selling their food and drink products abroad also face the same options. As knowledge of East Asian languages internationally is much less widespread than knowledge of English, it is relatively rare for brands to present their product in the original language without any transliteration. As foreigners are generally unfamiliar with East Asian writing systems, the majority of potential consumers will not even be able to read the name of the product. In the past, there was a tendency to create new brand names to appeal to Western audiences, as demonstrated by the high-profile case of the Japanese firm *Sony*. *Sony* was originally called *Tokyo Teletech*, but it changed its name to sound more natural to Western companies, adopting a new brand based on the 1950s slang term *sonny boys*, meaning 'smart young men'. However, from the 1980s onwards, Japanese companies have become associated with high-quality manufacturing. Accordingly, more Japanese companies began to use their transliterated Japanese names abroad, for example, *Toyota* or *Honda*. Another notable example is the beverage *Yakult*: according to the official website, "when he developed Yakult back in 1935, scientist Dr Shirota was keen to choose a name that could be understood globally, and so chose the word 'Yakult' from the 'universal language' of Esperanto".[7] However, nowadays, the average consumer is more likely to associate the word 'Yakult' with Japan, rather than Europe.

However, there are also some examples of companies presenting products using the original East Asian language, albeit alongside a translation. The figure below shows a box of Chinese-origin tea, purchased in the Netherlands, with trilingual packaging in Chinese, French, and English (Figure 5.8).

The English and French text on the box is a loose translation of the Chinese text. It is possible that one reason for the provision of Chinese text is for communication with the overseas Chinese diaspora. The Netherlands has a large Chinese immigrant community, with an estimated 51,000 first-generation Chinese living in the country in 2011.[8]

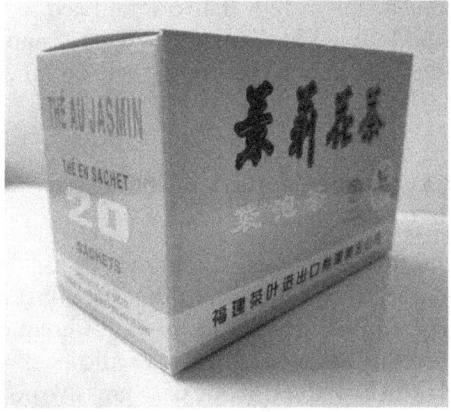

Figure 5.8 Imported Chinese tea in Leiden, the Netherlands.

In this way, multilingual branding allows the company to market their products not only to the majority population, but also to a significant minority culture of the country.

Nonetheless, there are many millions of people in the Netherlands who have no knowledge of the Chinese language, but these potential customers are also served in some ways by the use of foreign branding. The Chinese text is presented in a stylised, brush-style font, conveying the meaning that the tea is an 'exotic', authentic Chinese product, and thus an attractive new experience for Western buyers. In this way, the company skilfully uses the image of their COO and employs their cultural capital to boost overseas sales.

It is notable that despite the fact that the product was purchased in the Netherlands, the packaging features no Dutch text. Instead, English and French text is used, constituting yet another example of foreign branding. In this way, the product sellers take advantage of the fact that the Netherlands is a country with many multilingual inhabitants; an estimated 89% of the population has knowledge of English as an additional language, and 29% reported knowledge of French in 2012.[9] Indeed, previous research has suggested that Dutch consumers prefer English-language branding to Dutch-language branding, provided that the English text is not too difficult to understand (Hornikx, van Meurs, and de Boer, 2010). Additionally, Dutch customers have been shown to ascribe positive attributes, such as 'beautiful', to French language in advertising (Hornikx, van Meurs, and Starren, 2007). Accordingly, companies' marketers utilise foreign branding to take advantage of Dutch consumers' positive views of other languages and cultures, with the result that they do not need to translate any of the branding into Dutch. This shows how East Asian companies use their cultural linguistic capital to boost their commercial success in Western markets.

5.5 East Asian companies' foreign branding for a domestic market

It is also common for East Asian companies to use foreign branding for products that are only intended for domestic consumers. The availability of different English words to express different concepts, in addition to the words in the local language, allows speakers a greater expressive range. The expanded scope of expressive possibilities serves to enhance lexical power and becomes cultural capital to users (Hills, 2002). In many East Asian countries, the use of English can convey positive meanings to customers, such as trendiness, fun, or authenticity. The tone of branding materials and the ability to attract customers can matter much more than the grammatical 'correctness' of the text or its prepositional meaning.

Due to the importance of expressivity in branding, I propose both communicability and expressivity as criteria that can be used to explain companies' lexical choices. Lexical interaction inevitably creates common words that have a wide communicability. Yet, people also have a desire to express themselves in specific ways, or in specific styles. This results in the adoption or selection of words which may be less common, or based on elements from different languages, in order to produce the desired overall meaning. There are no objectively 'correct' answers when making lexical choices; stylistic variation plays an important role in these choices. One may question the appropriateness of a particular lexical choice, but this does not mean that it is 'incorrect'. Rather, the ability to choose between different words on the basis of the overall tone and meaning delivered is an important aspect of linguistic cultural capital. By presenting audiences with the most suitable words, companies project identities for their brands that individuals seek themselves to acquire, such as stylishness and cosmopolitanism.

When it comes to foreign-born or new words in general, local people tend to have a pick-and-choose mindset as consumers of these words, whereby they select those words or concepts they feel will be of most use to their goals, regardless of whether their use of these words subscribes to grammatical or conceptual conventions in the language of origin. Of course, consumers make the decision to purchase based on multiple factors, and branding plays a crucial role in influencing these decisions. Understanding advertisements requires a multi-modal understanding of the semiotic information given for the product. East Asian branding is particularly of interest as it can demonstrate the impact of complex lexical contact. Finding the right word for each situation is not easy and one needs to consider multiple factors, including situational context and target audience, in order to make the best lexical selection. Sometimes, people design new words for a concept or product, even if a commonly understood word for the concept already exists.

Designing a new word is a common practice in branding, but it is becoming increasingly visible in non-commercial areas too. In this sense, people act as creators and consumers of new words. Instead of using a new word's source-language meanings and forms (such as spelling and pronunciation), the consumers of words can pick and choose the word's forms and meanings as they see fit, reassembling and reinventing them in a natural localisation process. For example, some coffee shop names in Korea, like *Hollys Coffee* and *A Twosome Place*, do not make any sense to UK or US English speakers. Yet for Koreans who place emphasis on the use of English words and romanisation as a way to produce a modern and trendy feeling, the dictionary meaning of *Twosome* or the orthography of *Hollys* without an apostrophe is simply beside the point. These words have their origins in English, but in the Korean context they now have not only a different meaning and usage, but a form which would be seen as incorrect by many UK or US English speakers. The way the words' predecessors were used does not have any bearing on how they are used after a localisation process. Instead, the way that people understand and use them in the new context becomes the most important defining factor.

There is evidence that East Asian customers will consider domestic products more favourably if they erroneously assume a Western COO. In 2008, a study by Zhuang et al. examined the effects of Brand Origin Confusion (BOC) in China, finding that the effects are asymmetrical depending on the COO. To elucidate, based on data collected from 400 Chinese respondents, the authors found that local brands were more likely to benefit from BOC. That is, local brands benefited from being mistaken for foreign brands. This may account for some of the reasons for Chinese companies' eagerness to use English-sounding words in their domestic branding, such as *Clio Coddle* (a clothes store)[10] or *Helen Keller* (an eyewear company).[11] Sometimes, other East Asian countries even export English-language branding to China, benefiting from the country's enthusiasm for English names. The image below

Figure 5.9 BASICHOUSE MAN – English-language branding of a South Korean company at a mall in Chengdu, China.

shows a *BASICHOUSE MAN* outlet at a mall in Chengdu, China. While the brand name incorporates English words, it is actually a clothing chain that originated in South Korea (Figure 5.9).[12]

In South Korea, there is, similarly, a long tradition of using English words in branding. Originally, the use of English names was restricted to areas related to Western culture, such as restaurants serving Western food, bakeries, and boutiques (Lee, 1998). However, a decade later, this trend started to spread to other areas. When foreign words are used, the core meaning is transferred. However, it seems that, more importantly, marketers depend on the fashionable, trendy connotations of English words. In this case, the literal meanings of words are secondary. Hence, we see numerous names of Korean brands that may sound strange to English speakers. For example, the use of English in Korean café names is often nonsensical to English speakers, such as *Angel-in-us, caffe themselves,* or *connects coffee.*

In Japan, too, there is evidence that English branding is viewed as 'exotic' or stylish, as in South Korea. Holmquist and Cudmore (2013) conducted a study comparing the use of English in advertising in

Japan and the Philippines. The investigation found that English was highly prevalent in Japan, being present in 96% of advertisements and 42% of store fronts examined. The authors also concluded, on the basis of their analysis of survey responses, that the majority of Japanese respondents saw the use of English as an 'exotic' marketing strategy, or for businesses to show their international outlook. This contrasted with the situation in the Philippines, where English use was viewed as a way to attract international investment in the country. As in South Korea, the literal propositional meaning of brand names is often viewed as less important than their expressive connotations. Commonplace food and drink brands like *Pocari Sweat* (a sports drink), *MOS Burger* (a fast food chain), may therefore appear unnatural to native English speakers.

5.5.1 Case study – foreign branding in China

In this section, I provide a case study of foreign food and drink branding as used in China. Providing examples with photographs, I discuss how branding professionals have applied their linguistic capital.

5.5.1.1 Bobocorn

This popcorn snack on sale at a convenience store in Chengdu appears to have a brand name that is a compound of Chinese and English. The first element *Bobo* is from the Mandarin 抱抱 (*bàobào*, 'hug'), whereas the second element is the English word 'corn'. Through the reference to hugs and the cartoon character on the front, the brand exudes a cute image to appeal to its customers. The creation of a new compound word is emphasised through the tagline 'creative snacks' below, seeking to portray the snack as innovative – a common feature of English branding in East Asia. Furthermore, the Mandarin word for popcorn is 爆米花 *bàomǐhuā*; therefore, the use of *bobo* or *bàobào* (抱抱) is also a play on words connecting the *bào* in *bàomǐhuā* with the *bào* of a hug. The tagline at the bottom says 我要抱抱 *wǒ yào bàobào*, meaning 'I want a hug', but because of the use of *bào*, it also suggests 'I want popcorn'. This connection is not visible to consumers who cannot recognise Chinese characters, suggesting that the branding decisions, including the use of the English word 'corn', are collectively intended to appeal the product to potential consumers in a domestic setting (Figure 5.10).

120 *New words as cultural capital*

Figure 5.10 Bobocorn – popcorn in Chengdu, China.

5.5.1.2 Trilingual bread

The branding on the front of this packet of sweet bread, purchased at a Shanghai convenience store, contains elements from English, Chinese, and Japanese. The message reads *shēngchū mǎnmǎn yuánqì – níunǎi much bàng miànbāo* (生出满满元气 – 牛奶much棒面包), meaning roughly 'fills you with vigour – excellent bread with much milk'. The term *yuánqì* (元气, 'vigour') is a word deriving from the Japanese term *genki* (元気, 'vigour'), whereas the term 'much' is English. The incorporation of English and Japanese words perhaps seeks to portray the bread as exciting and cosmopolitan, boosting its appeal to the consumers of a globalised Shanghai, but it may also be a decision designed to piggyback off the popularity of Japanese pop culture in China and across East Asia, which has caused certain high-frequency Japanese words, such as *genki* and *kawaii*, to become translingual, global terms commonly understood within youth vernacular. In this way, the product can appeal in different ways both to those who are familiar with the Japanese language and culture, and to those who are not (Figure 5.11).

New words as cultural capital 121

Figure 5.11 Bread with English, Chinese, and Japanese branding in Shanghai, China.

5.5.1.3 Hand grasping cake

On Figure 5.12, the English product name 'hand grasping cake' appears to be a direct translation of the Chinese word *shǒuzhuābǐng* (手抓饼). While the English sounds unnatural to a native speaker, as if it were a cake that would come to life and grasp the customer's hand, it perhaps makes the product sound more exciting to a domestic audience. Similarly, the basic meaning of *hot* is easily expressible in Chinese, but is presented in English for stylistic effect (Figure 5.12).

5.5.1.4 Trilingual chicken

This signage contains words from English, Chinese, and Korean. Reading *H.O.T huǒ yàn zhájī chikin maekju* (H.O.T火焱炸鸡치킨맥주), it might be translated as 'hot flaming fried chicken fried chicken beer'. Note the repetition of 'fried chicken' due to the use of both the Chinese and Korean terms. While the literal meaning of the sign is somewhat hard to understand, it is rich in expressive meanings. The use of the English term 'hot' may appeal to the popularity of globalised products, represented by the Roman alphabet, whereas the inclusion of Korean words benefits from South Korea's international reputation for serving chicken with beer (Figure 5.13).

Figure 5.12 Poster at a fast food stand in Shanghai, China.

Figure 5.13 Trilingual signage in English, Korean, and Chinese.

5.3.1.5 u.loveit

This instant coffee packet, spotted at a supermarket in Shanghai, incorporates an English-style brand name 'u.loveit'. By incorporating the text-speech style 'u' and a full stop, perhaps reminiscent of URLs, the brand designers have made use of English elements to portray the product as modern and innovative (Figure 5.14).

5.5.1.6 Trilingual soda

This fizzy drink, bought at a convenience store in Shanghai, displays words from Chinese, Japanese, and English. The main brand name *yuánqì shuǐ – qīngguā wèi sūdá qìpào shuǐ* (元気水 – 青瓜味苏打气泡水) can be translated as 'vitality water – cucumber flavour soda carbonated water'. The term *yuánqì* (元気, 'vigour') is from the Japanese term *genki* (元気, 'vigour'), whereas the term *sūdá* (苏打, 'soda') is from the English term 'soda'. Non-transliterated Japanese text also appears on the bottle, detailing how the drink has no sugar, fat, or calories. Through this multilingual mix, the soda portrays a cosmopolitan, modern image to potential customers (Figure 5.15).

Figure 5.14 Instant coffee packet in Shanghai, China.

124 *New words as cultural capital*

Figure 5.15 Drink packaging with multiple languages in Shanghai, China.

5.5.1.7 *C'est bon*

The bottled water shown in Figure 5.16, photographed at a supermarket in Shanghai, has a brand name influenced by the French language. The brand name in Roman characters, 'c'estbon', is clearly influenced by the French phrase *c'est bon* meaning 'it is good'. The water, however, is sourced not from France but from within China, with the company being headquartered in Shenzhen. In contemporary China, French luxury brands can be an important part of cultural capital and are considered a status symbol by some, being particularly popular among the new rich ('nouveau riche'). Thus, it appears likely a French name was chosen to convey a sense of luxury and class to the company's domestic Chinese audience. However, the Chinese name of the water brand is *yíbǎo* (怡宝, 'happy treasure'); so the brand has not tried to transliterate the French phrase, but has translated some of the sense that it is 'good' (Figure 5.16).

New words as cultural capital 125

Figure 5.16 French-influenced bottled water in Shanghai, China.

5.6 Western companies' foreign branding for a domestic market

Similar to the use of English foreign branding in Asia, East Asian languages are used for branding purposes in many Western countries. In the UK, a prominent example is the *Superdry* clothing brand, which features on its products snippets of text in Japanese script. The actual Japanese text is often grammatically incorrect or incomprehensible to Japanese people. Nonetheless, the text appeals to many British consumers by making the clothing seem more modern and international, due to the Cool Japan phenomenon, and may also appeal to international fans of Japanese pop culture products. Japanese words transliterated into Roman letters are also used in food branding in the UK. Examples of popular restaurant chains in the UK include *Itsu* ('when' in Japanese) and *Wagamama* ('selfish' in Japanese). Although the literal meanings of these store names sound odd to Japanese speakers, most British consumers do not consider this to be terribly important. Instead, the expression of 'exoticness' is much more significant in the minds of the audience. As these restaurants use foreign words or scripts, it automatically leads consumers to feel they have an authentic experience with the cuisine and, by extension, with the culture that cuisine belongs to. In this way, the meaning of the language used in the source language is not a very relevant factor (Kiaer, 2019a).

The products sold by these restaurant chains also feature nonsensical East Asian terms. For example, the takeaway food shops *Wasabi* and *Itsu* feature a line of small pots filled with rice and toppings, which are referred to as *potto* and *potsu*, respectively. While *potto* is a fully fledged English-origin word in Japanese, appearing in authoritative Japanese dictionaries like the *Kōjien* (広辞苑), it is not normally used in this specific context. However, *potsu* is a completely made up word; the English term 'pot' has been joined with the Japanese syllable '*tsu*' to create a word which sounds more 'Japanese' than the English term alone, and which also harks back to the '*tsu*' in the brand name *Itsu*. Given that this word has no predefined meaning in either English or Japanese, it is not a hybrid word, but an entirely nonsensical term used to give a certain impression in the mind of the everyday Western consumer.

Hybrid words are also created by mixing terms from multiple foreign languages. For example, a Vietnamese restaurant in the UK sells a cocktail called *Phojito*, which appears to be a blended word combining the terms *phở* (a Vietnamese soup dish) and *Mojito* (a Cuban cocktail). In this case, not only is the literal meaning of the word hard to understand, but also it is not clear how it should be pronounced: should it be spoken like a Vietnamese word or a Spanish word? Nonetheless, the new word appears doubly exciting to consumers on account of its multilingual origin (see Section 3.4.3).

Recent research provides some backing for the idea that people in the UK have positive impressions of the use of East Asian Words (EAW). In the results of a survey of university students in Britain, You, Kiaer, and Ahn (2019) found that most students expressed a desire to learn more EAW and to use them in their daily communication in English. In addition, using EAW in English was seen as 'fun', 'exciting', 'useful', 'interesting', and 'brilliant'. This is potentially because the words are relatively new borrowings into the English language, making them seem exciting and innovative. Additionally, understanding of a geographically distant culture with different customs to one's own is likely to be associated with a high level of education. Thus, it is possible that the use of EAW could make the speaker appear more sophisticated. The precise factors which lead English speakers to view EAW positively is a potentially interesting area for future research. The results suggested that students were very open to EAW and keen to consider them as belonging not only to the language of origin but also to 'their' English, acknowledging them as dual identity words.

Outside of the UK, too, similar uses of East Asian foreign branding for domestic consumers are observed. There are examples of Japanese-style foreign branding in the Netherlands, too – such as an Asian supermarket called *toko*. Interestingly, the word *toko* is just a generic term for any kind of 'shop' in the Indonesian language, but it is now used in Dutch to mean 'an Asian supermarket' specifically. Presumably, Dutch people picked up the word either from Indonesian immigrants in the Netherlands, or while they were stationed in Indonesia during the colonial period.

Another example is a chocolate name branded as *Geisha* by a Finnish confectionary company. According to the brand's website, Geisha chocolate is intended to "bear traces of the mystique of the Orient", "aspire to something beyond the everyday", and "leave an imprint of Japanese culture". Despite the supposed Japanese origin of the biscuit filling and the product's cherry blossom-themed packaging, the relevance of the word *Geisha* is somewhat questionable as a brand name. Although it is in fact a Japanese term for a woman studying arts, singing, and dance, *Geisha* is known in the West largely as a term connoting a certain kind of traditional Japanese women's dress and make-up. Given its apparent lack of any connection to chocolate biscuits or confectionary of any kind, the word *Geisha* here is yet again being used as a signifier for Japanese-ness and to spark interest in the product's 'exotic' origins. Indeed, the use of exoticisation as a branding strategy appears to be commonplace in both the West and East Asia, but the impact of such branding decisions should be carefully analysed and understood within broader discourses of exoticisation and 'othering', which can perpetuate stereotypes and contribute to social exclusion.

5.7 Summary

In this chapter, I introduced the idea of linguistic cultural capital and explored how it is used in foreign branding, with a particular focus on East Asia and the West. I discussed how foreign branding is applied not only by international companies but also by local companies seeking to appeal to domestic consumers. Both East Asian and Western brands use foreign words from one another's languages to add a new and exciting flavour to their products.

Notes

1 www.oxfordreference.com/view/10.1093/oi/authority.20110803095652799.
2 https://dictionary.cambridge.org/dictionary/english/branding.
3 https://wired.jp/2018/02/07/history-of-a-verb-google-it/ (in Japanese).
4 www.oxfordlearnersdictionaries.com/definition/american_english/google.
5 www.pret.co.uk/en-gb/about-pret#.
6 www.bbc.com/news/world-asia-24140705.
7 www.yakult.co.uk/about-yakult/what-is-yakult (accessed 22nd December 2019).
8 www.cbs.nl/nl-nl/achtergrond/2011/17/ruim-51-duizend-chinezen-van-de-eerste-generatie-in-nederland (in Dutch).
9 https://ec.europa.eu/commfrontoffice/publicopinion/archives/ebs/ebs_243_en.pdf (p. 152).
10 www.seattletimes.com/business/chinese-retailers-play-a-creative-name-game-to-appear-foreign/.
11 https://blogs.wsj.com/chinarealtime/2012/04/18/are-those-helen-kellers-youre-wearing/.
12 http://tbhglobal.co.kr/ENG/HTML/03_BASIC.php.

Bibliography

Adams, J. (2017) 'English education in North Korea in the 1990s–2000s: the perspectives of two defectors.' In Jenks, C. and J.W. Lee (eds). *Korean Englishes in Transnational Contexts.* Palgrave Macmillan, Basingstoke. 221–237
Ahn, H. (2014) 'Teachers' attitudes towards Korean English in South Korea.' *World Englishes* 33(2), 195–222.
Bolton, K. (2003) *Chinese Englishes: A Sociolinguistic History.* Cambridge University Press, Cambridge, UK.
Bourdieu, P. (1985) 'The forms of capital.' *Handbook of Theory of Research for the Sociology of Education* (1986), 46–58.
Clements, R. (2019) 'Brush talk as the "Lingua Franca" of diplomacy in Japanese-Korean Encounters c. 1600–1868.' *The Historical Journal* 62(2), 289–309. doi:10.1017/S0018246X18000249.
Crystal, D. (2000) 'Emerging Englishes.' *English Teaching Professional* 14(1), 3–6.
Cummings, P.J. and H.G. Wolf. (2011) *A Dictionary of Hong Kong English: Words from the Fragrant Harbor.* Hong Kong: Hong Kong University Press.
Durkin, P. (2014) *Borrowed Words: A History of Loanwords in English.* Oxford: Oxford University Press.
Eckert, P. (2012) 'Three waves of variation study: the emergence of meaning in the study of sociolinguistic variation.' *Annual Review of Anthropology* 41(1), 87–100.
Edamame. (2019a) *Dinner.* [Online]. 2019. Edamame Japanese home cooking and sushi restaurant. Available from: www.edamame.co.uk/dinner [Accessed: 3 April 2019].
Edamame. (2019b) *Sushi.* [Online]. 2019. Edamame Japanese home cooking and sushi restaurant. Available from: www.edamame.co.uk/sushi [Accessed: 3 April 2019].
García, O. and W. Li. (2014) *Translanguaging: Language, Bilingualism and Education.* Basingstoke: Palgrave Pivot.
Grice, P. (1975) 'Logic and conversation.' In Ezcurdia, M. and R. Stainton (eds). *The Semantics-Pragmatics Boundary in Philosophy.* London: Broadview Press.

Grosjean, F. (2012) 'An attempt to isolate, and then differentiate, transfer and interference.' *International Journal of Bilingualism* 16(1), 11–21.

Hills, M. (2002) *Fan cultures* (Sussex studies in culture and communication). London: Routledge, Taylor & Francis Group.

Hong, F., A. Pecotich, and C. Shultz. (2002) 'Brand name translation: language constraints, product attributes and consumer perceptions in East and Southeast Asia.' *Journal of International Marketing* 10(2), 29–45.

Hornikx, J., F. van Meurs, and M. Starren. (2007) 'An empirical study of readers' Associations with multilingual advertising: the case of French, German and Spanish in Dutch advertising.' *Journal of Multilingual and Multicultural Development* 28(3), 204–219.

Hornikx, J., F. van Meurs, and A. de Boer. (2010) 'English or a local language for advertising?: the appreciation of easy and difficult English Slogans in the Netherlands.' *Journal of Business Communication* 47(2), 169.

Holmquist, John & Cudmore, B. (2013). English in Korean Advertising: An Exploratory Study. *International Journal of Marketing Studies*. 5. 10.5539/ijms.v5n3p94.

Hsieh, F. and M. Kenstowicz. (2008) 'Phonetic knowledge in tonal adaptation: mandarin and English loanwords in Lhasa Tibetan.' *Journal of East Asian Linguistics* 17(4), 279–297.

Itsu. (2019a) *Crushed coconut & chocolate oishi bar*. [Online]. Available from: www.itsu.com/menu/sides-snacks/crushed-coconut-chocolate-oishi-bar/ [Accessed: 3 April 2019].

Itsu. (2019b) *Sides, snacks & drinks*. [Online]. Available from: www.itsu.com/menu/sides-snacks/ [Accessed: 3 April 2019].

Japan Centre. (2019) *Wagashi Japanese Bakery Sweet Red Bean*. Available from: www.japancentre.com/en/products/3058-wagashi-japanese-bakery-sweet-red-bean-dorayaki [Accessed: 3 April 2019].

Kachru, B. (1985) 'Standards, codification and sociolinguistic realism: the English language in the outer circle.' In Quirk, R., H. Widdowson, and Y. Cantù (eds). *English in the World: Teaching and Learning the Language and Literatures*. Cambridge: Cambridge University Press.

Kachru, B. (1994) 'Englishization and contact linguistics.' *World Englishes* 13(2), 135–154.

Kiaer, J. (2014a) *The History of English Loanwords in Korean*. Munich: Lincom Europa.

Kiaer, J. (2014b) *Pragmatic Syntax*. London: Bloomsbury.

Kiaer, J. (2019a) *Translingual Words*. Abingdon: Routledge.

Kiaer, J., J. Guest, and X.A. Li. (2019b) *Translation and Literature in East Asia: Between Visibility and Invisibility*. Routledge Studies in East Asian Translation. Abingdon: Routledge.

Kiaer, J. and A. Bordilovskaya. (2017) 'Hybrid English words in Korean and Japanese: a strange brew or an asset for global English?' *Asian Englishes* 19(2), 167–187.

Kiaer, J. and S. Han. (2019) Multi-Modal Endings in Korean Instant Messaging: The Case of Korean Youth, Proceedings of *Association of Korean Studies in Europe*, Rome, Italy.
Kiaer, Calway, and Ahn (ms) Asian language inspired culinary terms in the English language: the case of Chinese, Japanese and Korean, University of Oxford.
King, R. (2015) 'Ditching "Diglossia": describing ecologies of the spoken and inscribed in pre-modern Korea.' *Sungkyun Journal of East Asian Studies* 15(1), 1–19.
Lewis, G., B. Jones, and C. Baker. (2012) 'Translanguaging: developing its conceptualisation and contextualisation.' *An International Journal on Theory and Practice* 18(7), 655–670.
Loveday, L. (1996) *Language Contact in Japan: A Sociolinguistic History*. Oxford: Oxford University Press.
Lurie, D. (2011) *Realms of Literacy: Early Japan and the History of Writing.*, Cambridge, MA. Harvard University Press.
Liu, L. (1995) *Translingual Practice: Literature, National Culture, and Translated Modernity; China, 1900–1937*. Stanford, CA: Stanford University Press.
Magnusson, P., S. Westjohn, and S. Zdravkovic. (2011) '"What? I thought Samsung was Japanese": accurate or not, perceived country of origin matters.' *International Marketing Review* 28(5), 454–472.
Moody, A. (1996) 'Transmission languages and source languages of Chinese borrowings in English.' *American Speech* 71(4), 405.
Muñoz-Basols, J. and D. Salazar. (2016) 'Cross-linguistic lexical influence between English and Spanish.' *Spanish in Context* 13(1), 80–102.
Myers-Scotton, C. (1993) *Social Motivations for Codeswitching: Evidence from Africa*. Oxford: Clarendon Press.
Myers-Scotton, C. (2006) Natural codeswitching knocks on the laboratory door. *Bilingualism: Language and Cognition* 9(2), 203–212.
Nord, C. (2001) *Translating as a Purposeful Activity: Functionalist Approaches Explained*. Abingdon: Routledge.
No, H. (2000) *Han- chung- il hanja ŏ-hwi pigyo: kaehwagi shin-ŏ wa shinyong-ŏ rŭl chungshim ŭro [Comparison of New Words in the Early 20th Century: The case of China, Korea and Japan]*. Masters Thesis, Kŏn'guk tae'hakkyo kyoyuk taehakwŏn.
Obento. (2019) *Takeaway menu*. [Online]. Available from: www.obento.co.uk/assets/images/menus/obento-takeaway-menu-web_v2.0.pdf [Accessed: 3 April 2019].
Office for National Statistics. (2013) '2011 census: key statistics and quick statistics for local authorities in the United Kingdom.' Available from: www.ons.gov.uk/peoplepopulationandcommunity/populationandmigration/populationestimates/bulletins/keystatisticsandquickstatisticsforlocalauthoritiesintheunitedkingdom/2013-10-11 [Accessed: 18 November 2019].

Ogilvie, S. (2012) *Words of the World: A Global History of the Oxford English Dictionary*. Cambridge: Cambridge University Press.
Seargeant, P. and C. Tagg. (2014) *The Language of Social Media: Identity and Community on the Internet*. Basingstoke: Palgrave Macmillan.
Seid, D. (2018) 'The "anti-hipster" feminism of Asian auntie cooking web series.' *Feminist Media Studies* 18(4), 779–782.
Schneider, E.W. (2007) *Postcolonial English: Varieties around the World*. Cambridge: Cambridge University Press.
Shibatani, M. (1990) *The Languages of Japan*. Cambridge: Cambridge University Press.
Tenshi. (2019) *HOT DISHES | Japanese Restaurant Angel | Tenshi | North London*. [Online]. 2019. Tenshi – menus. Available from: www.tenshilondon.com/menus-1 [Accessed: 4 April 2019].
Tenshi. (2019) *SUSHI | Japanese Restaurant Angel | Tenshi | North London*. [Online]. 2019. Tenshi – menus. Available from: www.tenshilondon.com/menus [Accessed: 3 April 2019].
Urquieta, P. (1973) *Estudios sobre Vocabulario [Studies on Vocabulary]*. Santiago de Chile: Editorial Andrés Bello.
Venuti, L. (1995) *The Translator's Invisibility: A History of Translation*. Abingdon: Routledge.
Vervotec, S. (2007) 'Super-diversity and its implications.' *Ethnic and Racial Studies* 30(6), 1024–1054.
Wagamama. (2019a) *Curry*. [Online]. 2019. Wagamama menu. Available from: www.wagamama.us/our-menu/curry [Accessed: 3 April 2019].
Wagamama. (2019b) *Sides*. [Online]. 2019. Wagamama menu. Available from: www.wagamama.us/our-menu/sides [Accessed: 3 April 2019].
Wagamama. (2019c) *Teppanyaki*. [Online]. 2019. Wagamama menu. Available from: www.wagamama.us/our-menu/teppanyaki [Accessed: 3 April 2019].
Williams, C. (2002) Extending bilingualism in the education system. *Education and lifelong learning committee* ELL-06-02.
Yang, J. (2009) 'Chinese borrowings in English.' *World Englishes* 28(1), 90–106.
YO! Sushi. (2019a) *YO! Sushi – Japanese Fried Chicken*. [Online]. 2019. YO! Sushi – menu. Available from: https://yosushi.com/menu/chicken-karaage [Accessed: 3 April 2019].
YO! Sushi. (2019b) *YO! Sushi – Kaiso Seaweed*. [Online]. 2019. YO! Sushi – menu. Available from: https://yosushi.com/menu/kaiso-seaweed [Accessed: 3 April 2019].
You, Z., J. Kiaer, and H. Ahn. (n.d.). 'Growing East Asian words in English: British university students' attitudes to words of East Asian origin in the English language.' *English Today* 1–18. doi:10.1017/S026607841900018X
Zhong, A. (2019) 'The top 100 Chinese loanwords in English today: can one recognise the Chinese words used in English?' *English Today* 35(3), 8–15.
Zhuang, G. et al. (2008) 'Asymmetric effects of brand origin confusion: evidence from the emerging market of China.' *International Marketing Review* 25(4), 441–457.

Index

ABC (American-born Chinese) 57
accents 9, 18, 30–31, 36
accessibility 16, 92
acculturation 14
adjectives 3, 6, 12, 33, 80
adverbs 33
advertisements 117, 119
aigre-douce 36
Ainu people 5, 42, 84
aircon 57
almond cream 57
android 106
Anglicisation 10, 16, 46, 52, 57, 102
Anglo words 27
Anglo-Indian 57
Anglosphere 73, 75, 77
anthropomorphisation 99
ants-climbing-a-tree 20
APP ('mobile application') 30
Arabic 2, 72
archaic 57
arroz bacalhau 63
arroz doce 63
Asian Americans 97, 99, 101
Asian auntie 99
Asian languages 19, 21, 26–29, 39, 42, 54, 57, 72–74, 100, 106, 114, 125
aunty 57
Australia 3, 46, 53, 60, 72–74
Australian English 6, 29, 34, 38, 47, 51–52
Austria 35
authenticity 8–9, 16, 48, 51, 95, 99–100, 102, 115–116, 126
azuki/red bean 23

bacon 2, 64, 90
banana 27, 57
banh mi 18, 33–34, 50, 86
bao 33, 63, 94, 119
baozi 33, 39, 90
bap 67, 88
batā 43
batā hōrensō 43
beef katsu 65
beef sashimi 16, 22, 34
beeru 39
Beijing 36–37, 62
Beijing duck 36
Bella Italia 107
Beogeoking 108
BGN/PCGN 1964 System 32
bibimbap 34, 67, 82–83, 86–87
bibimbap salad 67
bilingualism 74, 76, 79, 100
birth language 13, 25
bitter melon 57
blending 54–55
blog 99
boba i, ix, 97
Bobocorn 119–120
BOC (Brand Origin Confusion) 117
bokkeum 89–90
boomerang words 39–40
Bopomofo 31
borrowing 2, 10, 13–14, 28, 38–39, 41–44, 46, 57, 64, 72, 87–88, 127
boundaries 11, 14, 22, 72, 78
branding 10, 15, 104–107, 111, 114–121, 125–128

British English 6, 18, 48, 57, 94, 100
broccoli 2
brownie (bulangni) 30
bubble tea 64, 95, 97–98
bulgogi 16, 18, 34, 48–50, 83
bulgogi mvp 64
bulgogi mvp toseuteu 64
bungalow 57
Burger King 108, 111–113
buuz 20
buzz word 99

Café Rouge 107
caffè latte 61
calamari 13
calligraphy 33
calques 20, 22, 36, 41, 45–46, 52, 55, 65, 89, 91, 97, 110
Cambodia 24
Cambridge Business English Dictionary 105
Canada 3, 60, 72, 74
canard de Pékin 36
Cantonese 20, 28, 30, 36, 65, 72
Cantonese pinyin 30
Caribbean 18
carrot 2, 50
Celery 2
Central American Indian languages 2, 16
cha siu bao 94
chāhan 44
chang 34, 45
chanoyu 41
chao tom 34, 51
chăofàn 44
char kway teow 33
char siu 20
chawan 41
cheeky 57
Chengdu 118–120
chicken 57–59, 85, 121
chikin 58, 121
chilli/chili 16, 50, 79–80, 86
chilli powder 17
chilli sauce/chili sauce 16, 17, 50, 79
chimaek 58–59
Chinese cultural sphere/Sino cultural sphere 4, 26, 56
Chinese script 26

Chinese tapas 18, 68
chit 57
chocolate 2, 24–25, 110, 127
chong texse toxu qorumisi 85
chō'on 41
chop 36, 57, 21
chop chop 36
chop suey 33
chopstick 36, 47
chow mein 33
choy sum 33
chūnjuăn 46
Chuseok 108
chutney 2, 22
Classical Chinese 32, 56, 76
Classical Tibetan 31
clipping 57
Coca-Cola 107
code-switching 14, 22
coffee 2, 13, 27, 40, 61, 70, 111–112, 117–118, 123
cognate 41, 44
colonisation 3, 10, 13, 33
communicability 116
compounding 54–55
congee 57
conjunction 6
conservancy 57
consonants 32
consumers 104, 106–108, 110–111, 113–117, 119–120, 126–128
context 3, 5, 7–8, 10, 13, 16–18, 20, 23, 27, 47, 55, 61, 64, 68–71, 76–77, 79, 82, 88–89, 99–100, 106, 114, 117, 126
COO (Country-Of-Origin) 105–106, 111, 113, 115, 117
cooperative principles 8
core borrowing 13
coriander 50, 79
corpus 6, 38, 47, 54, 79, 92, 96
cosmopolitanism 120, 123
côtelette 88
count nouns 57
crystal bun 57
Cuba 60, 126
culinary terms 10, 12, 20, 25–29, 40, 58, 60, 63, 79, 83
cultural assets 11
cultural borrowing 13

cultural capital 1, 78, 83, 104–108, 110, 115–116, 128
cultural heritage 98
cultural identity 26
cultural transmutation 14
curry 24, 41, 43–45, 47–50, 56
curry house 49
curry rice 56
curry sauce 48–49
cutlet 39, 40, 65, 88
Cyrillic alphabet 4, 32

dashi 34
database 5–6, 34–35
deculturation 14
definite article 75
demographics 12, 54, 113
derivation 54–55
diacritics 10, 42, 86
dialects 28, 30
diaspora 7, 9, 72, 98, 100, 114
dictionary of scene language 35
Dindings 58
diversity 1, 3, 5, 52, 71, 76, 114
doenjang 34, 82
domestication 19–20
don katsu 40
dove 110
DPRK (Democratic People's Republic of Korea/North Korea) 4, 29, 32
Dravidian languages 72
Duden dictionary 34–35, 40–41
dumpling i, ix, 3, 17–18, 20, 38–39, 43–44, 52, 89–92, 94–96, 101
Duolingo 73
Dutch 16, 42, 70, 112, 115–116, 127

East Asia ii, 3–7, 10, 12–15, 18, 20, 26, 28–29, 51–52, 54, 56, 61, 71, 73–74, 76–78, 95, 104–105, 107, 112, 114, 119–120, 127–128
East Asian cuisine i–iii, x, 2, 5, 16, 33, 78–79, 98
East Asian Cultural Sphere 4, 75
East Asian markets 104, 107
EAW (East Asian Words) 126–127
ebook 6
Edamame 22, 24–25, 34, 41, 43–44
efficiency i, 7–8, 87

EFL (English as a Foreign Language) 3, 74–75
egg tart 21, 58, 63
ehomaki 69
ELF (English as lingua franca) 15, 71, 75–77
emoji 81
empathy i, 7–9, 68, 87, 89
English Fever 75
Englishisation 28
English-language education 29
English-origin words 13, 30–33, 42, 56, 79, 126
Enlightenment period 27
eomma 9
ethnocentrism 19
etymology 2, 19, 33, 67
exotic 24, 27, 70, 115, 118–119, 126–127
Expanding Circle 3, 6
expressive range 1, 83, 116
expressivity i, 7–8, 87, 116

fandoms 54, 82, 99
Fanta 110
feu 59
file attachment 82
Filipino 15, 72
Finland 127
first-generation words 6–7, 20, 26–29, 35–36, 38–39, 41, 44, 46, 51–52, 54–55, 58, 60, 70–71, 114
fish sauce 51, 79
foreign branding 104–107, 114–116, 119, 125, 127–128
foreignisation 19–20
Formosan 31
forms ii, ix, 1, 3, 6, 8, 11, 13–16, 18–21, 25, 27, 29–30, 35–36, 46, 52, 54, 56–58, 60, 62–65, 70–71, 73–74, 78, 86, 89, 95, 97, 102, 117
French 2, 10, 16, 33, 36, 39–40, 48, 50, 52, 59, 73, 88, 106, 114–115, 124–125
fry pan 56
fu yung 33
fugu 41
Fujian 57, 62
fusion 15, 54, 58, 67, 69–71
fusion cuisine 15, 54, 58, 69–70

gairaigo 42–43
galaxy 80–81, 110
galbi 36, 83
ganbei 27
Gangnam Style 73
gatekeeping 99
Geisha 127
genki 120, 123
German 2, 16–17, 34–36, 38, 40, 52, 73, 88, 95
gimbap 36, 86–87
global branding 10, 15
global English 7, 55, 84, 89, 106
global exchange 72
global lexicon i, 71, 78–79
Global Web-Based English 6, 38, 54, 66
global words 7, 16, 54, 70–71, 80, 102, 106
globalisation 10, 25, 58, 71, 79, 102, 107
GloWbE 6, 38, 47, 51, 54, 66
gnocchi 94
gobo 34
Goethe-Institut 35
goma wakame sarada/goma wakame salad 44
Google 5, 62, 88–89, 94, 106
Google Books 5–6
Google N-gram 6, 21, 36, 92, 96
Google Trends 6, 49, 59–60, 62
grammar 29, 56, 60, 83
grammatical variation 83
grapheme 109
gravy 48
Greek 2
Gricean maxim 8
Guandong 57
The Guardian newspaper 22
guotie 92–94
gyoza 20, 24, 34, 39, 43, 44, 91–92, 94

haemul 8
haiku 28
Hakka Chinese 31
half-romanisation 24
half-translation 24
hallyu 15, 73, 82
hamburg steak 65
Han China 4

Han Dynasty 62
handwriting 30
Hangul 32, 109
Hanyu Pinyin 30–31
hànzì 26, 109
har gow 94
hashtag 6, 50, 86, 88, 92
Heineken 112
Hepburn system 22, 31, 41, 46
Hershey's 110
high heel 56
Hindi 2, 72
hiragana 31
Hmong 72
hoisin 33, 38
Hokkien Chinese 2, 31, 62, 64
homogenisation 91, 102
Honda 114
Hong Kong i, ix, 4–5, 9, 12–13, 21, 29–30, 38, 47, 55, 57–58, 63, 65, 67, 94
Hong Kong English 29, 38, 47, 57
Hong Kong Examinations and Assessments Authority 30
Hong Kong Government Cantonese Romanisation 30
hot pot 18–20, 46–47
hot-and-sour 20
hot-pepper paste/Korean pepper sauce 20–21, 83
hotto doggu 42
Huawei 106
hybrid words 7, 54–57, 76, 126
hybridisation 15, 60–61, 71, 90
Hyundai 105

ice tea 56, 70
identity 15, 22, 26, 40, 62, 68, 89, 98, 127, 132
ideology 14
imperialism 12
imported words 13–14, 16, 28, 39
India 3, 48–49, 57, 72
Indic script 31
indigenous minority 5, 31, 84
Indonesia 3, 127
Inner Circle 3, 6, 14, 56
Instagram 50, 78, 84, 92, 94
interjection 6
international trade 12, 15

Index

internationalisation 3
internet 21, 77–78, 83
internet forums 77
iPhone 80
IRF (initiation-response-follow-up) 98
IT 78
Italian 2, 16, 36, 61, 72–73, 94–95
Itsu fast food chain 24–25, 126

Jamaica 94
Japan i, ix, 3–5, 9, 12, 15, 23, 26–28, 31, 34, 38, 40, 42–43, 47–48, 55–56, 62, 65, 67, 74–77, 84, 92, 105, 107–110, 114, 118–119, 126
japchae 83
Jiaozi 20, 33, 39, 44, 91–94
Jjigae 19
journals 6, 34
J-pop 3, 54
JSTOR 5–6, 58

kaiseki 34
kaisō 25, 41
kaki 41
kalbi 36
kalguksu/knife cut noodles 89, 91
kanji 31
karaoke 36
karē 41, 43, 48
kari/karil 48
katakana 31, 42, 62, 65, 109
katsu 39, 40, 43, 65, 88
katsu curry 43
katsu don 40
katsu karē 43
katsuretsu 88
kawaii 120
kēki 42, 62–63
ketchup 2, 33, 42, 48
Khmer 72
kimbap 36, 83, 86
kimuchi 43
Knödel 38
kochujang/gochujang 20–21, 34, 67, 83
kombucha 41
Korean BBQ 36
Korean sushi 36
Korean wave ii, 15, 21, 73, 82

K-pop 3, 54
kuaizi 36
Kuala Lumpur 58

La Tasca 107
language borders 14, 25
language contact 12, 14, 27–28, 55, 60, 74–75, 77, 102
language purification movements 29, 55
Lao 72
Latin 2, 31, 40
latte 61, 70
letter duplication 25, 41–42, 64
lexical borrowing 13
lexical interaction 10–12, 15, 116
lexical migration 13
lexical power 1, 83, 116
lexical variety 13
lexicography i, 13, 16, 19, 34, 83, 86
li 33
li ting 33
lingua franca 3, 15–16, 26, 71, 74–77, 102
linguistic authorities ix, 7, 10, 19, 29, 70, 83, 102
linguistic capital 104–105, 110, 116, 119
linguistic currency 3
linguistic environment 11, 15
linguistic heritage 98
linguistic minorities 9
loan 13–14, 42, 57, 89
loan translations 57, 89
local words 29, 71, 99, 106
logograph 109
long vowels 31, 41

Maangchi 99–100
Macao 4
Macquarie dictionary 6, 34, 36, 38, 45–46
macron 41–42, 86
maekju 58–59, 121
magazines 35
maguro 34
maki zushi 34
makkoli 34
makudonarudo 108
Malacca 57

Malay 2
Malayalam 72
Malaysia 4, 50, 57–58
Mandarin 28, 30–31, 44, 63–65, 72, 76, 85, 95, 106, 110, 113–114, 119
mandu 20, 39, 91–92, 94
mango 57
manti 8, 24, 39, 41
Mao-tai 33
marketing 15, 24, 105–108, 119
marmalade 1–2
mass nouns 57
matcha 25, 34, 46–47, 61
matcha latte 61
McCune-Reischauer system 32
McDonald's 108
meanings ix, 1, 3, 8, 11, 13–16, 25, 29, 38, 52–53, 58, 71, 80, 83, 88, 95, 97–98, 102, 113, 116–118, 121, 126
Meiji era 31, 48
Meiji restoration 28, 39
Merriam-Webster dictionary 6, 34, 38, 48, 59
Mexico 16
Micronesia 72
Middle Chinese 46
Midori 34
mien 33
migrants 7, 12, 48, 54, 57, 72, 127
milk tea 21, 65–67, 95, 97
mini-flat 57
mini-hall 57
Ministry of Education and Statistics 75
minority cultures 78, 84
minority voices 16
mirin 34
miso shiru 19, 25
miso soup 19, 25
mizutaki 34
mochi 34
Modern Standard Mandarin 30
modernisation 28, 56
mojito 60, 126
momo 34, 39, 44
Mongolia i, ix, 4–5, 9–10, 12, 20, 26, 30, 32, 47, 84
Mongolian (language) 4, 20, 26, 30, 32

monolingual/monolinguals 31, 100
moo goo gai pan 33
moo shu 33
moon cake 45, 55
Moon Jae-in administration 75
morphemes 30
MOS Burger 119
MTR (Mass Transit Rail) 57
mukbang 100
multilingual 3, 13, 72, 76, 105, 107, 115, 123, 126
multi-modal 16, 117
mutsu 41

Nahuatl 2
National Institute of Korean Language (NIKL) 55–56
national language 32, 56, 74
nation-state 4, 11, 14–15, 22, 26–27, 83
natto 34
Netherlands 70, 114–115, 127
netizens 19, 78
newspapers 6, 19, 34–35, 56, 59, 83
Nexis 5–6
niwatori tōage/Japanese fried chicken 23
non-verbal communication 78, 80
noodle 2–3, 10, 17, 25, 38, 41, 50–51, 59, 64, 89, 91, 94–95
nori 5, 9, 16, 31, 34, 78, 84–85, 115
noun 3, 6, 9, 12, 23, 28, 33, 36, 48, 57, 64, 80, 106, 126
nuance 8, 10, 68, 99
Nudel 38
number marking 57
nuoc mam 34, 51

obsolete words 35
ohaw 84
oishi bars 24
ojingeo 8, 13
okonomiyaki 34
omakase 34
omochi 34
omuraisu 42, 65
omuretsu 42
onigiri 23
online communication 72, 99

online lexicon 6
Oriental 91
orthography 19, 117
othering 127
Ottoman Turkish 2
Outer Circle 3, 55
Oxford English Dictionary (OED) 2, 6, 16, 18–21, 27, 33–36, 38, 44–51, 58–59, 61, 65, 82, 88, 91, 106
oyakodon/parent-and-child rice bowl 22–23

Pacific Island languages 72
pad-thai 24
painappuru kēki 62–63
pajeon 8, 83
Pan-Asian 18, 20, 24, 46, 57, 91–92, 99
pancake 8, 34, 38, 46
Pan-East Asian 26–27
panko 34
Pasteis de Nata 63
pastel de nata 65
PCEs (Postcolonial Englishes) 13
Pėh-ōe-jī 31, 62
Peking duck 36, 38, 55, 79
Penang 58
Pepsi Cola 110
Philippines 72, 119
pho/phở 10, 18–19, 50–52, 59–60, 126
pho salad 59–60
phojito 56, 60, 126
pierogi 94
piggy bun 63
pineapple 62
pineapple cake 21, 58, 62–63
pizahatto 108–109
Pizza Hut 108–109
Pocari Sweat 119
politeness registers 105
Polynesia 72
ponzu 34, 70
pop culture 78, 82, 120, 126
popcorn 119–120
popular culture 15, 73, 83
pork bun 63
pork chop 21, 58, 63
pork chop bun 58, 63
pork katsu 40

portmanteau 42
Portuguese 2, 10, 16, 30, 40, 42, 44, 48, 62–63, 65, 73
Portuguese Egg tart 63
potato 2
potstickers 92
potto 126
pragmatics 8
PRC (The People's Republic of China)/mainland China 4–5, 9, 12, 30–31, 58, 62, 76
prefix 24, 55
preschool 75
prescriptivism 97
prestige 56, 105
Pret a Manger 106
print media 78, 83
private education 74–75, 105
pronunciation 9, 16, 22, 27–28, 32, 36, 42–44, 60, 83, 100, 102, 110, 117
ProQuest 5–6
Punjabi 72
puns 16, 51, 72

QQ 64
QWERTY keyboards 21

raisu 42–43, 65
raisukarē 43
ramen 34, 41, 87
ramyen 87
ramyeon/ramyun 87
ravioli 39, 94
recipient language 16, 27–28
Red Bull 110–111
reduplication 99
register 22, 83, 105
Republic of Korea (South Korea) 4, 8, 21, 32, 58, 64, 70, 74–77, 105, 108–110, 118–119, 121
Revised Romanisation 21, 32
rice 5, 18, 22–23, 38, 42–43, 45, 48, 50–51, 56, 59, 64–65, 67, 80, 82, 86, 88, 126
rice burger 18
ROC (Republic of China) 4
romaji 31
Romanisation 1, 10, 18–24, 30, 31–32, 36, 41–44, 52, 117

Romanisation of Korean system 32
root-for-root translation 22
Royal milk tea 65, 67
Russian 32, 73, 79
Russian alphabet 32

saké 18, 34
salad 44, 59–60, 67
samla curry 24
sāmon furai/samon furai 43
Samsung Galaxy 80–81
samurai 36
sarada 44
sashimi 16, 22, 34
satay/satay sauce 50
satsuma-age 40
scientist 27, 114
Scottish clootie dumplings 39
seaweed 22, 25, 41, 44, 86
Second World War 76
secondary school 31, 73–74
second-generation words 7, 14, 16, 54–60, 70–71, 73, 102
seitan 33
self-study 73
semiotic primitives 14
semiotic repertoire 13–14
semiotics 13–14, 117
sencha 46
Seupaem 108–109
7 up 112
shabu-shabu 34
sheng jian bao 94
shiitake 41
shiru 19, 25
shiso 34
shochu 34
shoyu 19
shrimp twigim 68–69
shu 33, 62
shumai 33
shushu 9
Sichuan region 5
simplification of forms 78, 86
simplified Chinese 30
Singapore 3–4, 57–58, 62
Singaporean English 47
Sinitic 4, 26–27
Sinitic-origin 26–27
sinographic cosmopolis 26

Sinosphere 4, 26
siu mei 20, 33
Skopos theory 20
smartphones 30, 78, 106
soba 34
social landscape 1, 21–22, 83
social media i, ix, 1, 3, 6, 10, 15–16, 19, 29, 34, 54, 64, 71, 77–80, 82–89, 91–92, 94–95, 97–102
social media post 78–80, 82, 85–86
social status 105
sociolinguistics 1, 13, 21, 83
sociology 104
soda/fizzy drink 123
soju 34, 59, 82
somaek 58–59
Sony 114
sophistication 127
soup 10, 19, 25, 41, 51–52, 59, 126
source language 20, 24, 42–44, 86, 117, 126
South Korea 4, 8, 21, 32, 58, 64, 70, 74–77, 105, 108–110, 118–119, 121
South-Eastern Asia 4
soy 16, 18–19, 25, 33, 41, 46, 49, 70, 82
soy sauce 16, 19, 70
spacing 21, 31
Spam 108–109
Spanish 2, 16, 40, 68, 73, 126
Special Administrative Region 4
spring roll 46
squid 8, 13
Standard Romanisation 30
Starbucks Coffee 110–112
stereotypes 127
stir-fry 20
Straits Settlements 57
styles (linguistic) 1, 13, 16, 21–22, 116
stylishness 116, 118
subculture 6, 15
subgum 33
subtitles 100–102
suet dumplings 39, 94–95
suffix 55
suimono 34
sukiyaki 34
sunomono 34

Superdry 125
sushi burrito i, ix, 18, 69
sweet-and-sour 16–17, 20, 33
Switzerland 35
syllabary 22, 31, 109
Szechuan 33

Tagalog 72
Taiwan 4–5, 31, 58, 62–64, 67, 74, 76, 95, 97, 113
Taiwanese Mandarin 31
Taiwanese Romanisation system 31
Tamil 48, 72
tapas 18, 68
tapioca pearls 95, 97
target audience 10, 117
tataki 34
tea 1, 25, 41, 44, 46, 56, 61, 64–67, 70, 95, 97–98, 114–115
The Telegraph newspaper 73
Telugu 72
Temaki/hand roll 22
tempura 24, 34, 40, 68
teppan-yaki 34
teriyaki 34
texts 30, 32, 34–35, 58
Thai 24, 72
Third Wave (of sociolinguistic theory) 1, 13, 21, 83
three Es model 7
Three Kingdoms period 62
Tibet 31, 34, 45
Tibetan 30–31, 33, 44–45, 84
Tibetan Pinyin 31
tihm syun 20
toast 27, 63–64
TOEIC 105
tofu 16, 18, 28, 33, 46
tofu bulgogi 16
togarashi 86
tomato 2, 42
ton katsu 40, 65
tone markers 10, 86
tones 10, 18, 30, 86
toro 34
tortellini 94
toseuteu 64
tourism 76–77
Toyota 114
traditional Chinese 30, 62–63

transculturalism i, ix, 1, 10–11, 14, 15, 29
transculturation 14
translanguaging ix, 14, 78–80
translation i–ii, 1, 8–10, 16, 18–25, 27–28, 36, 41, 54, 57, 62, 65, 70, 89, 100–101, 106, 110–114, 116, 121, 123–124
translation theory ii, 19–20
translingual i, ix, 10–16, 18, 20–21, 23, 25, 29, 35, 38–40, 44, 46, 52–53, 58, 70, 78, 83, 89, 98, 120
translingual identity 89
transliteration 1, 19–22, 24–25, 30–31, 36, 43, 49, 106, 108–114
transnationalism i, ix, 14–15, 29, 76–77, 83
trend 6, 14, 19, 28–29, 35, 49, 59–62, 73, 82, 91, 99, 116–118
trilingual 114, 120–123
tsampa 34
T-shirt (T xu) 30
tsukemono/pickle 22–23
tsunami 28
Turkish 2, 79
tūsī 63
Twankay 33
twice-cooked pork 20
Twitter/tweet 6, 16–19, 21, 39–40, 45–47, 52, 59–60, 64, 67–69, 78, 82, 84–87, 89–93

udon 34, 108
Uighur 85
UK 1–3, 10, 15, 22, 24–25, 29, 34, 38, 41, 47–49, 53, 59–60, 64, 72–74, 76–77, 88, 102, 106–107, 110, 117, 125–127
UK English 38
umami 34
umeboshi 34
UN (United Nations) 4
unagi/freshwater eel 25
universities 73–74
UNTWO (World Tourism Organization) 76–77
US English 6, 38, 117
USA 3, 16, 33, 48, 53, 60, 72–74, 76, 97
Uyghur 30

variant 38, 86–87, 89
variant spelling 86–87
vegan bulgogi 16, 18
veganuary ix
verbs 12, 33, 35, 43, 106
Vietnam i, ix, 4–5, 8–9, 12, 32, 34, 38, 75
Vietnamese 4, 8, 10, 15, 18–19, 32–33, 46, 50–51, 59–60, 72, 86, 126
Vietnamese mint 46
Vietnamese spring roll 46
viral hit 73
vlogging 98–101
vocabulary 12, 19, 29, 52–54, 73, 100, 110–111

Wade-Giles system 30
Wagamama 24, 43–44, 126
wakamame 34
Wasabi 126
wasei eigo 42–43
water-cooked meat 20
Wei 62
Weibo 101
Western culture 10, 118
wine 27
wok 33, 79

won ton 33
word variants 98
word-making 3, 16, 55
World English(es) 1, 3, 6, 15, 36, 99
World Wide Web 77
Wu 62
Wylie transliteration system 31

yaki 20, 34
yaki nori 34
yakisoba/thin buckwheat noodles 25, 34
yakitori 34
Yakult 114
Yale romanisation 30
yasai 24
yoghurt 2
yokan 34
yōshoku 39, 65
YouTube 98–101
yuan hsiao 33
yuèbǐng 45
yuzu 70
yuzu ponzu sauce 70

zen water 24
Ziphian law 8

For Product Safety Concerns and Information please contact our EU representative GPSR@taylorandfrancis.com
Taylor & Francis Verlag GmbH, Kaufingerstraße 24, 80331 München, Germany

www.ingramcontent.com/pod-product-compliance
Lightning Source LLC
Chambersburg PA
CBHW051749230426
43670CB00012B/2220